You Can Still Live

You Can Still Live
*A Monthly Companion to Help You
Experience the Best of Your Life*

By:
Rebecca L. Chauncey

You Can Still Live – A Monthly Companion to Help You Experience the Best of Your Life

Copyright © 2015 by Rebecca L. Chauncey

All rights reserved.
ISBN 10: 1517250927   ISBN 13: 978-1517250928

No part of this book may be reproduced, distributed, or transmitted in any form or by any means, including photocopying, recording, or other electronic or mechanical methods, without the prior written permission of the publisher, except in the case of brief quotations embodied in critical reviews. Unauthorized reproduction of any part of this work is illegal and is punishable by law.

Book Design and Edits: Jalyne Strong-Shaw
Author Photo: Images and Visions by S. Glover LLC

First Edition
Printed in the United States of America.

Contents

Acknowledgments   7

Introduction   9

Anytime
  The Beauty of Unfolding   12
  Do You See It?   15
  You Are Not Alone   18
  Your Touch   21
  Yesterday   23
  True Inspiration   26
  Power   29
  No Hurry for Love   32
  What Do You Really Need?   34
  Looking Forward   36
  Plants Are Gentle Teachers   39
  Higher   41
  Peace for You   44
  Twenty-First Century Love   47
  You Know   50
  Woo   53
  Your Own Way   55
  Shine and Share   57

Beginning of Year
  Join Me and Believe   62

Contents

The Miracle of Love	65
Thank You	68
We Must Hold On	71

Spring

Love and Patience	76
Embrace Expressions of Love	79

Summer

Love Conquers All	84
Turn Worry Into Wonderful (July)	87
Moving (end of summer)	89
Everything and More	92

End of Year

Golden Teardrops Bring Freedom	96
Growing Up	99

Acknowledgments

I am very grateful for the opportunity to encourage people in verbal and written forms. Thank you, Precious Creator, for blessing me with the gifts to do so! I also thank you for guiding me to connect with wonderful teachers (like Universal Lightbearers) at ideal times to help me walk on my spiritual path confidently and graciously.

I greatly appreciate you, Jalyne! You are a superb designer, editor, and listener! As always, it is a pleasure working with you.

Thanks to Clayton and Kim for sharing book publishing knowledge with me. I also thank Tiffany for enlightening discussions about book publishing and marketing. May you all continuously experience great success!

Mom and Dad, thank you for your constant encouragement, support, and unconditional love! Mom, I especially thank you very much for continuously encouraging me to walk in my greatness!

To Lori: Thanks for being my dearest friend since the first grade! I also thank you for being a great sounding board for my business ideas, sharing your e-Reader, and cheering me on during the publishing process of my first best-selling book!

To AAT: Thank you for inspiring me in caring and sensible ways to live a fulfilling life and share my gifts with the world in ways that I truly enjoy! No more waiting, right? I'm making it happen now!

To Allison: You are an amazing wordsmith! Thanks so much for helping me brainstorm and tweak an important part of the book. I greatly appreciate you!

Special thanks to Barbara, Cethy, Dad, Jazmine, Leah, Nate, and Sharnele who said, "When is the book coming out?" I'm happy to say that it's here. May it be a wonderful gift for you and readers worldwide!

Thank you very much to everyone who has crossed my path as you have enhanced the way I appreciate life!

And I truly thank you, Dear Reader, for purchasing my book. May it help you at the perfect times to cherish your life, move forward with ease, and remember that "You Can Still Live!"

> Much appreciation, love, and peace!
> Rebecca

Introduction

Your life experiences can cause you to cheer, cry, laugh, shout, and wonder what to do next. The variety of feelings that you have can change in a day, week, year, or moment. How do you feel now? How is your week or year going? How can you make your life better?

You Can Still Live simply helps you see how valuable you are and how to live with more ease, keeping your busy schedule in mind. It is set so two letters are read monthly: one anytime, one seasonal – with six bonus anytime messages to read when desired. The Seasonal sections include: "Beginning of Year," "Spring," "Summer," and "End of Year." Some parts are dated with timeless messages that you can embrace any year during the respective seasons. Additionally, you can use the "My Insight" section after each letter to write your thoughts about how a particular message applies to your life.

The letters serve as brief, kind companions on your life journey to help you appreciate the beautiful parts of yourself and your multifaceted life. And you learn ways you can still live and better your life in the midst of challenges like dealing with negativity, moving forward after loved ones pass away, overcoming relationship changes, and working in frustrating settings.

Business owners, employees, students, and others have greatly appreciated how *You Can Still Live* reminded them of their power to keep living and move forward regardless of situations.

A corporate businesswoman says, "I've been dealing with work matters and my family just buried a beloved uncle. This puts everything into perspective; thanks so much for sharing this!"

A government employee says, "Absolutely beautiful. Your thoughts and way with words truly have touched my heart. Lately, I have been going in and out of 'funky moods.' Some days are better than others, but your words really hit close to home."

A healthcare businessman says, "Thank you for sharing your powerful testimony about men and life. I welcome repeatedly reading your work. It possesses a personal observation driven by truth, strength, passion, and love."

You see how others benefit from the authentic, heartfelt words that this book offers to help them live well. Now it's your turn! It's time for you to move through challenges easier. It's time for you to celebrate what's right in your life. It's time for you to smile again. It's time for you to fully trust yourself and the amazing power you possess. It's time for you to keep reading and apply the insight you receive from each letter. You will gladly enjoy how the book speaks to you in perfect ways and reminds you that "You Can Still Live!"

Anytime

The Beauty of Unfolding

Greetings!

Do you follow a tight schedule? Do you change your daily routine sometimes? Are you open to revising your plan if a new opportunity arises? While your answer may vary for each question, I encourage you to partake in a day that plays out freely very soon. There is much beauty in letting a day simply unfold because it creates excitement, helps you stay open to possibilities, and may include other unexpected pleasures.

The beauty of a day naturally unfolding is exciting. Have you ever received an unexpected call from a loved one asking you to join in something fun? I imagine that you felt excited about the opportunity. Recently, I was thrilled to receive a call from my sister to celebrate my birthday, months after it had passed. I was honored that she still wanted to do something special for me. I decided that my original plans for the day could wait while I seized the moment! You can do the same the next time someone calls or texts you about doing something unplanned.

Allowing a day to progress easily helps you stay open to possibilities. For example, you and a friend may suddenly decide to have lunch. During lunch, one of you is inspired by your conversation to travel to a community you have never visited. Traveling to the area and viewing its amazing architecture can inspire you to get a new home. Then, your friend may feel the urge to buy the car he or she always wanted after seeing that car parked in front of the well-designed house. Do you see how the possibilities expanded after you and your friend let the day flow easily? How nice is it that an impromptu lunch sparked wonderful possibilities!

Letting a day play out is also beautiful because it can include unexpected pleasures. I experienced this during the surprise birthday celebration I mentioned earlier. My sister and I started the day enjoying a delicious brunch. Then, we drove along the waterfront with the windows down and sang fun songs together. As we sat at a stoplight, the sight of people flying colorful kites delighted us. We also went to a botanical garden that has waterfalls and fragrant flowers. While there, we were amazed to see two animals we had not seen before: a lovely bird sitting in a tree and a furry animal that swam in the pond. These unexpected pleasures were nice to enjoy as our day naturally unfolded. How many unexpected pleasures will you note on your upcoming, free flowing day?

Are you ready for the beauty of just letting a day unfold? Of course, you are! You deserve to indulge yourself in such a day as it creates excitement, helps you open up to possibilities, and may include unexpected pleasures. While you have various matters to handle regularly, please give yourself the treat of enjoying new adventures without advanced planning soon. You and your loved ones will thoroughly enjoy the rewards!

> Loving the Beauty of Easy Unfolding,
> Rebecca

My Insight

Do You See It?

Hi, Wise One!

Do you see the amazing help that is regularly available to you? Some times help is boldly visible, while other times help is subtle. However, we can see all available help with a bit of practice and by using our wisdom. Please open your eyes and mind to learn how helpful messages can appear in the sky, through the animal kingdom, and on various signs.

Have you noticed the formation of clouds during the day or the cluster of stars at night when you look up at the sky? If you look closely, the clouds may form the shape of a door reminding you to walk through an open door to a great opportunity. Or the twinkling of stars may encourage you to shine brightly in your work and life. Stop for a while and look at the sky. Then, ask yourself, what information does the clouds, stars or sky as a whole want to share with me now?

Help may also be found by noticing the presence of the animal kingdom. Do you see butterflies fluttering pass you? Do you see geese stepping across the street? Or have you seen a rabbit hop along your path? These creatures provide helpful messages, such as the butterfly showing you the importance of moving through your life with ease. One day, I was relaxing along the lake front and two ducks sat near me. I wondered what message they had for me. Several minutes later, the words: relax, flow, support, came to mind. The message was timely as I was working with some frustration. I realized that the ducks were showing me the need to just flow, relax, and know I'm well supported in life. Observe when these or other animals come your way as they can convey the essential help that you need when you least expect it.

Have you ever seen signs that miraculously speak loudly about your life? Billboards, license plates, and t-shirts are just a few examples of these signs. They have extraordinary ways of helping you form new ideas or solutions to life's questions. For example, I was driving and saw a billboard that said, "Be empowered." I questioned what to do earlier that day, and the sign reminded me to continue working on my dreams. Another instance of a helpful sign was a license plate I saw while waiting at the stoplight. It read: Lov u 2RL. I screamed joyfully at that sign because RL are the initials of my first and middle names. It was wonderful to see that the Universe loves me. How many signs will help you today? Keep your eyes open and embrace the supportive omens!

There is amazing help available to all of us when we look. Let today be a great opportunity for you to receive assistance on your life's journey that may come from the sky, animals or signs, or all three. Stay tuned to your surroundings and see what messages await you!

Gratefully Seeing Signs,
Rebecca

My Insight

You Are Not Alone

Hi, Dear Heart!

There are times in your life when you will tell others that you feel fine, but deep down you do not. You may feel overwhelmed by your responsibilities or you are tired of doing the same things. You believe you are alone in your feelings and begin to think no one understands. I'm here to tell you that you are not alone! No matter the situation, you are never truly alone.

It is very nice to know that you and I are not alone. One morning, I woke up to that message on my mind. It was beautiful to hear as I was feeling so-so about my life. After the message: "you are not alone," came to mind, I instantly felt free of the thoughts that burdened me. The Creator blessed me with a gentle and sweet reminder that the Universe always has my back and I can let go of the challenges.

Sometimes you may feel engulfed by life's responsibilities. At these times, you can remember that you are not alone. Also, it is okay to accept help from others at times. You may feel like me and not want to hassle anyone, but, in actuality, we serve one another all the time. The key is to not wear out our welcome when people bless us with their generosity. They want us to feel loved and supported in the best ways, and we can simply be grateful when they do so.

After a long and tiring day, you may feel alone because there are things you have to do and help does not seem to be available. Fortunately, the Universe keeps us going as we evolve. Have you ever felt a sudden burst of energy when you initially felt exhausted? That was the Universe refreshing you to move forward instead of sleeping at your desk.

Are you convinced that you are not alone? With beautiful angels, delightful people and experiences in your life, you are not alone. Most importantly, we can be successful and supported in numerous ways. The Universe, loving people, and your true self love you, so live freely and fully knowing you are not alone.

Thankful We Are Not Alone,
Rebecca

My Insight

Your Touch

Greetings!

The meaningfulness of touch varies greatly. Some touches make you squirm, while others bring relief. But when it comes to your touch, nothing compares to it! Your touch is unique; it can be life-giving and very powerful when filled with love and sincerity.

Have you thought lately about the magnificent uniqueness of your touch? Take a moment to think about it. You already know that no other person in the world is exactly like you. Moreover, no one can touch someone or something in the same way as you do. How beautiful is that? Your unique touch can make certain people smile from ear to ear. Your unique touch can also make a meal or project just right.

Your touch can be life-giving. A life-giving touch helps restore the health of babies and adults alike. It helps pets feel at ease and lively, too. It is especially nice to witness a person who feels that he or she cannot move forward have a change of heart after receiving a life-giving touch from a compassionate person like you.

Your touch is very powerful when filled with love and sincerity. Have you hugged someone recently? Do you think love and sincerity was felt by the recipient? I hope so! That kind of touch, whether it is a hug, a handshake, or a kiss, lets the receiver know you care and want the best for him or her. If you have not touched someone with love and sincerity recently, bless someone dear with it today! And if you have done it recently, please do it again today!

What a marvelous touch you possess! It is unique. It can be life-giving. It is also very powerful when filled with love and sincerity. Let everything and everyone you touch receive your best. Then, you will certainly make a positive impact on the world!

Share Your Unique Touch!
Rebecca

My Insight

Yesterday

Greetings!

Do you remember everything that happened yesterday? Do you recall every detail about last week? Do you find that you dwell on old matters that do not add joy to your life? Answering yes to any of the questions presents a great opportunity for you to leave yesterday, enjoy today, and expect that the best is yet to come!

Yesterday unfolded in a certain way, but we do not have to keep replaying it in our minds. This is especially important to know if you are dwelling on matters that do not add joy to your life. You may have been upset in past moments, but that feeling does not have to carry into your new moments. Your life is too precious to stay stuck in past disharmony. You change your mind by being grateful for overcoming old situations, and then move forward in excitement about new days.

In fact, enjoying a new day is a wonderful way to let go of yesterday. When you wake up, smile and tell yourself that you will experience ease, peace, love, clarity, and productivity throughout the day. As the day unfolds, you can play a game with yourself and celebrate how each of the aforementioned characteristics shows up in your life. A baby may smile at you, which adds love to your day. Or you may complete several tasks with ease and excellence that equates to great productivity. As you embrace more things that go well and even how you overcome challenging moments, you are celebrating the now, and you can be happy about what is to come.

Being excited about what is to come is another significant way to let go of yesterday. You have a beautiful imagination to tap into at any moment. Can you imagine taking a trip to a country that you always wanted to visit? Can you see yourself living in a state-of-the-art home? Or can you see yourself working in joyful ways and receiving perfect cash flow to live beautifully? I can imagine these situations for you and me. Take time to think, feel, and see yourself in delightful experiences. In turn, your excitement about what is to come takes hold and yesterday is left behind.

Yesterday served its purpose in the past, so let it remain there. You are truly deserving of new, wonderful experiences! So be grateful for making it through yesterday, celebrate today, and be thrilled about the great experiences to come!

Free of Yesterday and Celebrating Today!
Rebecca

My Insight

True Inspiration

Greetings, True Heart!

Look around you. Do you like something you see? Do you admire someone around you? Or do you simply like how you're feeling right now? These are wonderful questions to ask yourself to discover what truly inspires you.

Understand that true inspiration can come from something you see. Noticing the bright blue hue of a clear morning sky may motivate you to take more outdoor walks. Seeing mistreated animals on TV can inspire you to volunteer at an animal shelter. Viewing a panorama of mountains or a big city skyline may inspire you to do more traveling. The images of some things can surely move you to want to do things differently.

People can inspire you to behave in certain ways. When a sweet toddler helps you complete household chores you may be inspired to finish the tasks with more joy. Watching family members laugh heartily during dinner can motivate you to fully enjoy the present moment with them and host more gatherings. Seeing the huge grin on your significant other's face when you say, "Hi (insert name)," may inspire you to share your most positive energy with him or her more often. People certainly have remarkable ways of inspiring one another.

True inspiration also comes from your own feelings. Being excited about a new day can help you get out of bed with a smile and give you the confidence to make the day your best yet. If you've felt frustrated for a few days, you may be inspired to move in a new direction that could bring more joy to your life. Your feeling of "knowing" that something or someone great is entering your life soon inspires you to keep trusting your instincts when others doubt it.

True inspiration can come from a number of things. Whether you see something or someone, or have a certain feeling, inspiration can move you in the most amazing ways. Who or what inspires you today? Answer that question and then let true inspiration carry you to beautiful experiences!

Inspired By Most,
Rebecca

My Insight

Power

Greetings!

Power comes in many forms. There is electrical power to light a room. There is mechanical power to build things. There is technological power that allows computers to conduct several functions simultaneously. Most importantly, we are fortunate to have power flowing through our beings to enhance the world. When you truly understand this fact, your life unfolds in phenomenal ways.

Like the electric power that can light up a room, you possess power of illumination. Have you ever been in the presence of someone who adds much delight and warmth to a room? Or have you been told that you radiate those qualities in a space? It is especially refreshing to interact with a person who shares uplifting power when others are decreasing delightful power with their negative comments or complaints. Light up more places with your peaceful, loving power!

The mechanical power that can build things is also inside you. You are full of power to create things, such as: a thriving business, an invention, or a beautiful room in your home. When you focus on creating something with full trust in the Creator and your soul, you can make one of a kind and life changing things. When was the last time you developed something? Build something with your machine-like power!

The technological power that enables computers to function is amazing. Similarly, have you thought about how great power flows through everyone? This is demonstrated when people around the world unite to send loving thoughts and money to help those in dire straits like those who have lost everything in hurricanes, tornadoes, floods, fires or other disasters. Power becomes mighty when everyone combines their best energies to transform mankind in positive ways. Imagine everyone doing so more often without needing a disaster as a catalyst. What a magnificent gift that would be for humanity!

How powerful do you feel now? Remember, you and I have the power to light up rooms, to build great things, and the power to unite with all people to demonstrate the mighty force of our combined energies! Walk in your full power regularly and see how much more radiant life becomes!

Powerfully,
Rebecca

My Insight

No Hurry for Love

Greetings, Love!

Are you wondering what your future love life will bring? Have people asked if you are married with children yet? Are you tired of being single? These questions can bring different feelings to mind. Regardless of your answers, I encourage you to not hurry love – romantic love, specifically.

When I consider my answer to being questioned about my future love life, I embrace the phrase: You can't hurry love. Let me say it again: You can't hurry love! I'm sure that you can think of at least one couple that knew each other at an early point in their lives, but didn't establish a long-term relationship until years later. Various circumstances in their individual lives transpired to help them to be eventually in a space to connect in a high quality relationship. Embrace that thought for a moment, and realize that there really is no need to rush being in a love relationship. Once you and your future love partner are really free in mind, body, and spirit, the beautiful and wise Universe will connect you two in the perfect way!

Some people may ask you if you are married with children. It's a simple question, and you don't have to take offense when it's directed to you. You can answer yes or no without detailed explanation. Or you can give an explanation without attaching emotion to it, such as: I am not married and do not have children yet. Or you may explain: I don't desire to marry or to have children. Remember, your life is yours. Living your life the way you feel best trumps what others think about you.

When you're single, sometimes you feel tired of not being in a relationship or not having a companion. But you must know that true and everlasting love is within you and surrounds you. Have you ever walked along a beach or other waterfront and experienced pure peace and happiness at the sight of the waves of water? That's love. Have you awakened with an unexpected feeling of growth to new levels and smiled? That's love. Has someone picked up an item you dropped for you? That's love. Have you appreciated the smile of someone walking toward you on the street? That's love. Isn't it wonderful that you can experience love whether you are in a romantic relationship or not?

Being questioned about your love life, or marriage and children plans, and your feelings about being single do not have to wear you down. Be mindful of the fantastic love within you and that surrounds you regularly. Before you know it, you will feel filled with love. Then, when you least expect it, that high quality, long-term relationship that you desire (but did not hurry) will be presented. Trust, and know it is done!

Grateful for Love Within and Without,
Rebecca

What Do You Really Need?

Greetings!

People commonly list food, clothing, and shelter as needs for survival. Some people would add that they require great health, financial resources, and love to live successfully. Have you thought lately about what you really need to live well? Let's explore a few types of needs and you can determine where yours fall.

One kind of need relates to flourishing. What do you need to flourish? Of course, flourishing goes beyond doing the same routine each day. It calls for you to know what's needed to thrive in life. You may need to have close connections with loved ones and do the work that you're passionate about to really flourish. Or you may need to flourish by living in a community that celebrates diverse cultures and respects all residents.

Another type of need includes peace of mind. Do you need a certain number of hours of sleep to remain peaceful? Do you enjoy peace when driving along a scenic route? Or do you need to sit on the couch and be by yourself for a while to maintain inner peace? No matter how you answer, peace can be need for living well.

The third kind of need relates to love. What do you truly need to love? You may need to exercise regularly or have monthly spa visits to give yourself love. And you may find that you need your significant other to show you love by spending uninterrupted time with you or sharing thoughtful gifts.

Thinking about what you need to flourish, be peaceful, or experience love is your uniquely individual experience. Carve out time to ask yourself sincerely, what are your needs to live well. Identify your particular survival needs today, and know that you deserve to have those needs met!

Fulfill Your Needs and Live Well,
Rebecca

My Insight

Looking Forward

Greetings!

*I*s the slow unfolding of your day or week dragging you down? Or is everything flowing just right and you're excited about what's to come? I hope the latter question describes your situation. There is something beautiful about looking forward. Let's discuss a few reasons for that feeling.

Looking forward helps us maintain excitement in life. When was the last time you were excited about a life event? If it's hard for you to remember when, please consider how you can change that now. For instance, you may look forward to any one or more of the following activities: eating a delicious meal, meeting friends you haven't seen in a long time, dancing with your love while wearing a new outfit that he or she has never seen on you (wow factor), traveling to a different city or country, or buying your favorite treat from the grocery store. You can create a list of the things, small and large, that you can look forward to today, this week or within the month. That new list will surely help add excitement to your life.

Looking forward allows us to imagine new possibilities for our lives. Are you pleased with current situations in your life? You probably feel pleased in some ways and not so much in others.

Spend time by yourself and think of new adventures you would like to enjoy in the near and distant future. Maybe you want to eat lunch away from your desk for a week. You may want to meet family members more often to participate in new experiences together. Or you may plan to visit one new city on six different continents within the year. Why NOT imagine taking an excursion of that magnitude? You are deserving of all the best in life, so go for it!

Looking forward helps us to walk safely! That statement may seem silly, but it's true. Have you ever walked down the street while looking behind yourself and maintained balance? I doubt it, my dear!

My point is that our bodies are built to keep us looking forward, and we can apply that concept to everyday living. Walking while facing forward keeps your body aligned, able to walk with ease and safely navigate. Remember this point whenever your thoughts cause you to dwell on past negativity. Shut that voice down and think about how much easier you can advance when you look forward.

Now, do you feel the importance of looking forward? You and I can maintain excitement about life, imagine new possibilities, and embrace the design of our bodies when looking forward. Let's be beautiful examples of people who look forward and live with more vitality!

> Joyfully Looking Forward,
> Rebecca

My Insight

Plants Are Gentle Teachers

Greetings!

Do you have a plant in your home or office? Did you grow up with plants in your home? If you can say yes to either question, you are very fortunate. If you answered no, join me and learn why plants are some of life's most gentle teachers.

Plants teach you the power of resilience. A great example of a plant's resilience is when it doesn't develop new leaves, but still doesn't die. I feel that when a plant is in this position it instinctively knows it will grow in due time.

Plants can also show you the importance of the right energy. I have a plant that my mother gave me that initially only had a few leaves on one stem. With some sunlight, water, and much love energy, the plant has grown and sprouted many offshoots! While sunshine and water clearly help the plant's vitality, my daily talks of thankfulness, love, and playing positive music have helped my plant grow abundantly.

Plants teach us to appreciate life. Do you know the variety of air pollutants that plants filter or the number of toxins they remove? It is phenomenal that plants do so much without asking you for assistance! If you do not have an indoor plant, you might consider getting one. If you have one or more, thank your plants for helping you breathe easier so you can appreciate life more.

Are you ready to give your plant a hi-five for all it does? Maybe not, but you can definitely thank your plant for teaching you the power of resilience, the importance of the right energy, and for helping you appreciate life. While plants gently teach you these amazing lessons, you, in turn, can demonstrate the same qualities to all people.

So Grateful for Plants,
Rebecca

My Insight

Higher

Hi, Gifted One!

Do you feel stagnant? Or are you climbing to a new level in life? Or are you already on a higher level of being? Your answers to these questions can serve to guide you to go higher in life. Celebrate going higher in multiple ways to enhance your life.

While you may feel stagnant in one or more aspects of life, you still have the ability to go to a higher level. You can take time to read more and hone a skill to help you climb to a higher level at work. You may also decide to exercise more and gain a higher percentage of muscle. Stagnation may appear at different points in your life, but you can overcome it.

Perhaps you are climbing to a new level in life. You know this to be true when you start to act differently to prepare yourself for something new. An example of this is when you're only getting four hours of sleep nightly and you notice that you tire easily, long before your bedtime. Then, you change your sleep schedule so you get seven hours nightly and you gradually feel more energized until bedtime. With continuous increased hours of restful sleep, you will go to a new level of feeling more refreshed to fully enjoy experiences and interact more patiently with others.

If you are already at a higher level of being, congratulations! You are maintaining behaviors that make you feel zestful or freer to be your true self. One instance of this is when you take ten minutes to sit still and simply breathe a few times a week versus an old habit of continuous attachment to electronics and doing too many things without getting needed rest, which caused burnout.

Now that you have a clearer understanding of what going to higher levels means, where are you? If you feel stagnant, commit to do something new. If you are between levels, keep climbing higher and know that victory is around the corner. If you have reached a new level, keep great momentum and celebrate your move to higher ground. Let's go higher a bit each day and inspire others to do the same!

> Climbing Higher,
> Rebecca

My Insight

Peace for You

Greetings!

Are you familiar with the hand signal for peace? Yes, I am talking about the two fingers positioned in a V-shape in the air! Many people display this signal in photos or flash it as they walk away. That is symbolic, however, real peace can be profoundly experienced in mind, body, and soul. Look at these examples of finding peace to see where you already have it or where you can expand it.

Peace of mind is beautiful and life-enhancing. Do you feel peaceful as you read this message? I hope so. If not, may it help you relax. Peace of mind will allow you to focus beautifully on one thing, such as reading or spending time with a loved one, without being distracted by other matters. With peace of mind, you trust that everything works out for your highest good. Thus, you don't get bogged down by feelings or thoughts that cause chaos in the mind. Look for ways to consistently embrace a peaceful mindset.

Peace in the body is crucial to sustaining your well-being. Steady, normal breathing and engaging periodically in deep breathing sessions maintains peace in the body. You can also experience a state of peace when sitting still. Take one minute to sit still and breathe, now. It is a great way to achieve peace in the body. Celebrate peace in your body before you go to bed and when you awake each day. Simply smile, then inhale and exhale, for sweet rest to come or in gratitude for rest enjoyed.

Have you felt peace in your soul? This can happen when you leave a place of hectic energy to spend time walking in nature. You can experience peace in your heart when hugging a loved one. And peace in your soul can be felt after you make decisions that you know are right for you. Peace in your soul helps you go the distance in life.

Peace can be profoundly experienced in your mind, body, and

soul. No matter what takes place today, carve out moments to experience peace in these ways. You will be able to enjoy peace in your life that is much more meaningful than a simple hand signal.

Stay Peaceful!
Rebecca

My Insight

Twenty-First Century Love

Greetings!

What do you feel when you see the word: LOVE? Does it make you think of family, friends, a significant other, or all three? Do you imagine a beautiful experience that makes you smile? Or do you think about an everlasting emotion? Whatever your thoughts on love are, it's fair to say that you felt it at some point in your life. So now I challenge you to embrace 21st century love.

There are a number of ways to experience 21st century love. One way is knowing that 21st century love always flows. You can experience this love when the sun shines on your face and makes you feel delightful and warm. You can also sense 21st century love while lying in bed feeling grateful for your home and wellbeing. Of course, this love is exemplified when your soul is at peace and you are filled with true "knowing" that all is well taken care of in each moment.

Another sign of 21st century love is living passionately. An expression of this love can be a chef preparing an exquisitely artful meal and describing the dish with great happiness. Living passionately displays 21st century love when a person travels to various countries and marvels at the cultures and beautiful people throughout the journey. And living passionately magnifies 21st century love when families laugh, talk, and play together in a free flowing exchange that makes everyone know they are loved.

Lastly, 21st century love is clearly demonstrated when you love yourself. Loving yourself with 21st century love enables you to stay home to relax regardless of the many events taking place one night. Or you take a class you always wanted to in spite of someone saying it would be silly to go. You also exhibit 21st century love when you love yourself enough to understand your true desires and gifts.

Twenty-first century love is truly the same as traditional love; you and I determine the ways it is displayed. At its core, LOVE connects everyone in the most beautiful ways. How many more ways can you experience love today? Go forth and enjoy them!

Endlessly Loving,
Rebecca

My Insight

You Know

Greetings, Brilliant One!

*Y*ou know many things. You know how to: tie your shoe, hug someone, and cover your mouth when you cough. The things you know go way beyond what's mentioned here, but consider this question: Do you always trust what you know, especially when it is not obvious to others? You truly have to answer this for yourself. To help you better answer that question, let's examine situations where your knowing trumps all.

There are times when the way you normally travel needs to change for various reasons. Sometimes there is an accident on the road or the train you are taking is packed. At such times do you suddenly think, "I ought to go take another route or a different mode of transportation?" Hopefully, you follow your knowing to make the necessary change to arrive at your destination safely and on time. Trusting what you know when traveling is important; it can save your life.

Your knowing is significant when determining which school to attend or what vocation to pursue. You or someone you know has probably picked a school or job because a family member said it was best. I hope that choice was best for you or the other person. Oftentimes, people experience stress and unhappiness because they did not trust their knowing about the ideal school or work opportunity that made their heart sing. Conversely, think of the excitement and bliss people display when attending a school they chose after visiting and feeling themselves going to class there. Or you may recall people who love their work when they do it. What you know to be the best school or professional opportunity for YOU counts the most!

Trusting what you know is also critical when choosing the best love partner. Think of a time when you or a loved one wanted a relationship with a particular man or woman and others could not understand why. While dear friends and family members generally mean well, they may not understand the deeper connection you have with a significant other. As long as the man or woman you choose to be with is not harming you, it is perfectly fine to establish or grow the relationship. With peace within your heart, you easily know who is best to be with you or who is not.

You know how to travel accordingly, you know the right school or work for you, and you know the right love partner for you. You know these things and much more. You feel peace, ease, love, and joy when trusting what YOU know, especially when it is not obvious to others. Go for what you know and trust the Universe to support you every step of the way!

Trusting and Knowing,
Rebecca

My Insight

Woo

Sweet Greetings!

*W*oo! Woo! Woo! Say it three more times: Woo, woo, woo! Repeating that expression provides you with a great sensation of relief, right? It is also a fun way of breathing and reminds us of the beauty of the breath. The gift of breath is marvelous because the simple act of breathing can ease you; help you to focus, and gives life.

Did you feel rushed going somewhere today? Did someone cut you off in traffic? Whether you were aware of it or not, I imagine that in either situation, you would have taken a deep breath. That conscious or unconscious action would have put you at ease, at least for the moment, and helped you to calmly move forward. There are many other examples of how breathing brings ease. Take note of your "easing" breaths today.

Breathing also helps to bring focus. You may measure your breaths carefully to stay focused throughout a presentation. Collecting your breath to focus on blowing out candles is common. And of course, breathing deeply to focus on the present moment helps tremendously. Encourage yourself to take a few deep breaths to focus during each day.

Do you know the main reason why breathing is a marvelous gift? Every day you wake up is a reminder of the power of breathing. From a good night's rest to a nap, waking up and breathing shows that you are alive and have another opportunity to experience the very best of life.

Breathing is a wonderful gift that can ease us, help us focus, and connect us to life. Keep this reality in mind when you're in traffic, at work, are alone — in all situations.

Breathing Easy,
Rebecca

My Insight

Your Own Way

Greetings!

Are you making decisions to build or maintain an average life or a life you really desire? At some point, you have to make decisions to live dynamically in spite of what you may be told by others. So what keeps you from making decisions that infuse your life with dynamism?

It is possible for all of us to live active and purposeful lives. Have you taken the time to ask yourself what living dynamically means to you? If you have, I'm glad to hear it! If not, take as much time as you need to sit in a quiet space and ask yourself the question, and listen to what comes to mind that excites you or resonates with you.

Oftentimes people get preoccupied with getting through the day, dealing with a mundane task or challenge. Then, they may forget the dreams born in their hearts years ago. However, beautiful dreams await your return so you can see them come to fruition. What dreams are waiting for you to decide to act on now?

Today is the perfect day to take control of your life's dream and live it enthusiastically. You can make the decision on your own to release mediocre ways and live with passion. Be free of doubts and despair and live your own way. With the Creator's help, you will make wise decisions to build and maintain the life of your dreams. Go your own way with confidence and watch how dynamically things come together!

Living Dynamically and Faithfully,
Rebecca

My Insight

Shine and Share

Greetings!

Are you ready to be resplendent and shine brightly today? Or does your inner light feel dim? No matter your answer, I'm thrilled to say that you can shine brilliantly! I often tell people that our lights are way too bright to keep from the world. So, let's discover how you can consistently shine your light on the world or return to shining brightly after feeling your light dim and the importance of sharing your light.

One of the nicest ways to shine brilliantly is when you do it consistently. You may feel that's easier said than done, but I imagine that you shine your light more often than you recognize. Have you sent someone a text saying hello or simply shared an emoji? You were shining your light. Have you smiled and expressed thankfulness for making it through the workday? You shined your light. Have you recently made a special meal or completed a project? You shined your light then, too.

As you move through the day, note on the "My Insight" page following this letter the numerous ways you shine brightly and encourage yourself to add more light in the world daily.

The second way to demonstrate resplendence is to brighten your light after feeling it dim. There are times when you feel confused, frustrated, or tired. I imagine that everyone has felt these ways at different points in their lives. Fortunately, you can spend time alone, breathe deeply, take a nap, walk outside and bask in fresh air, or talk with a confidant to turn up your inner light. You will gain the clarity, energy, and strength to start shining brilliantly once more.

It's great to shine your light consistently or begin again after feeling it dim, but do you know why it's important? Each time you glow by smiling, demonstrating your talents, or saying kind words to others, you add positivity to the world. This is significant because the light and warmth you radiate can encourage people to do the same (even if only for a few moments). Furthermore, sharing your beautiful light can help lessen the dim and dark situations in society. Think about it. If more people felt their bright light and power within, they would develop more respect for themselves and society.

Now you are truly ready to shine and share your light on the world! You've learned to account for the many ways to be resplendent consistently and how to renew the radiance of your light. You also know why it's important to shine your light and share it with all. In turn, the world will sparkle more brightly and positively.

Shine and share your light regularly,
Rebecca

My Insight

Beginning of Year

Join Me and Believe

Hi, Believer!

I'm greeting you this way because I want to encourage you to believe (FOR REAL) that your life and the lives of others can be much better. Do you believe it? If you answer with a hearty, "Yes!" then I truly hope that you will join me in thinking and acting this way throughout the year.

I want to speak life into your situations and motivate you to do the same with people in your circles, and those circles of friends will spread the news to others and so on. With all the negativity in the world, we need to believe in peace, blessings, excellent health, plenitude, success and ALL the good things that the Creator wants people throughout the world to have or experience.

Do you have great plans for 2009? I know I do! I am so thankful that I finally have a strong understanding of the Creator's purpose for me so I can plan accordingly. One purpose has come to my mind from time to time since 2006. When the initial idea first occurred I started working on it. Then, I worked on it intermittently until I eventually stopped. I guess I didn't fully believe that I could do it. A lack of belief may partially be the reason why my second dream was not developed more in 2008. Whether I saw something on TV or talked to certain people, I received confirmations to make my second dream come true. However, I didn't start to really believe in that dream until the end of 2008.

Now that 2009 is here, I am wholeheartedly believing in dream achievement and listening to my heart as the Universe equips me with what it takes to make my dreams come to fruition. It's so crucial that you and I believe in our dreams, and trust that the Creator will bless us with EVERYTHING we need to make them come to light.

Currently, there is talk of recession, depression, wars, fighting, killings, diseases, and more. While I know that these issues are real today, I believe that we can overcome them and do better. Let's talk more about abundance, peace, happiness and the good things that each of us is doing, or can do, so that everyone has more belief, and does better for themselves. Do you believe this is possible? I hope so. President Barack Obama knew the importance of belief as he inspired us to say, "Yes, We Can." Remember? What do you believe is true now?

I know what I'm going to do: Keep listening to my inner spirit and do what I'm meant to do with my life. I will also believe that MUCH MORE happiness, excellent health, love, peace, and prosperity is in store for everyone. May you fulfill your dreams and embrace the concept that everyone's dreams can come true!

Loving and Believing,
Rebecca

My Insight

The Miracle of Love

Greetings!

I hope this message finds you embracing immense gratitude and love on Valentine's Day. In support of the holiday and great love for every day, I encourage you to know that love and miracles continuously prevail in life. Take note of where you feel love right now.

Some people feel a great loss if they no longer work in a particular field, if they don't have a valentine, or if they're not in a romantic relationship. Instead of feeling down about these situations, we can remember that there are miracles to come.

The voice of love calls me when I get caught up in old thoughts that tell me that I can't move through a challenging situation or I won't have a wonderful romantic relationship. I had great romantic relationships before. However, after my last one, I let thoughts of doubt invade my mind causing me to believe that I wouldn't love that way again. Thankfully, I eventually changed my mind. Now I only accept thoughts that are good for me, such as: I'm having a new romantic relationship that is amazingly right for me and my man-to-be.

Once I stopped feeling the need to throw love away, beautiful miracles became commonplace in my life. The miracle of loving myself and staying committed to being a better person daily has allowed me to blossom and believe in romantic love again. The miracle of truly being open to a romantic relationship has developed, too. It doesn't matter that a previous relationship or work opportunity ends. There are great new miracles in store for me and anyone else who is open to the best opportunities and willing to embrace love of self and all people.

Are you dwelling on thoughts that love only comes in one form or from one person? Replace those old beliefs with new ones in which you fully accept unconditional love for self, for all people, and for the right partner and right opportunities to come.

Make the choice to operate in unconditional love on Valentine's Day and every day. The world will be so much better with everyone operating in unconditional love regularly.

Much love and all the best,
Rebecca

My Insight

Thank You

Greetings!

I celebrated my early March birthday all month long. Some of my friends teased me because it seemed excessive to celebrate for so long. In reality, it was a perfect way to become more grateful for life and its many blessings. Blessings can be great or small, and they appear in both blissful and challenging times.

Have you ever felt like you had enough? Some life experiences try to get the best of us, but we should remain grateful that the Creator blesses us with love and knowledge to guide us through to brighter days. For instance, while I was happy celebrating my birthday throughout the month of March, two of my friends' relatives passed away and another friend's loved one was diagnosed with a life threatening illness. You may think that it would be too hard to stay thankful when facing those last two situations. Yet those are times when it's most important to be grateful. When loved ones pass away, you can recall and appreciate the precious moments you spent with them. If someone becomes ill, it's a perfect time to really focus on the goodness of life and stay hopeful to experience healthier days.

At times it may seem that life is too tough to handle, but we should be thankful that we have the power to overcome. No matter what happens in your life, be excited and thankful that you're equipped with everything you need to thrive. I can think of times when life seemed unbearable. Thankfully, at these times something would eventually prompt me to develop solutions to resolve an issue. That "something" is one of many ways the Universe delivers us from seemingly unbearable moments. The Universe also has a way of reminding us of what we should appreciate during those times.

In fact, there is much to be thankful for in life, including: the Creator, food, clothing, safe/clean/secure home(s), supportive family and friends, a sound mind, a healthy body, the ability to hear/think/speak/breathe/walk/bathe/jump independently, smiles, laughter, money to share with others/save/pay bills/maintain livelihood, unexpected money when you really need it, sunshine, safe travels, employment, a new business venture, a new career opportunity, an unexpected call from a loved one you haven't heard from in a while, hearing your favorite song at a party, hearing a song that reminds you of someone special, a visit with a friend you haven't seen in a long time, traveling to a new city/state/country, restoring a weary body/mind/soul, a smile from someone on a tough day, strength to stay focused, the ability to only think positively despite the criticisms of others, getting a fresh haircut or hairdo, throwing a party that everyone enjoys, laughing at inside jokes between you and a friend, a hug or kiss from a loved one, a text message from a friend that simply says "How are you today?" when you initially felt down, Summertime (the season/the classic Fresh Prince song), the ability to walk down the street without watching out for bombs, prayers that are instantly answered, prayers that are answered when you least expected, and inner peace.

The thank you list can go on and on. Why don't you create your list now? I'm confident that you will be encouraged to move forward expecting more blessings and greater strength to live a wonderful life. Let's commit to be more thankful daily and encourage others to do the same. Each day of life really is a blessing and despite occasional challenges, we should always say "Thank You!"

Committed to Stay Ever Thankful,
Rebecca

My Insight

We Must Hold On

Greetings!

Have you ever felt like you should be doing more with your life? Are you striving to keep your thoughts only centered on positive things, but past hurts or lies creep into your mind causing you to think negatively?

At some point, you will question what you should really do or have in life. Once you truly realize what you should do or possess, you will most likely embark on your new path with good intentions. Unfortunately, just as you focus on your new endeavors, negative thoughts lead you to doubt yourself. Then, you may ask yourself, "How can I get over this?" The answer is simple: Hold on!

Are you trying new things now? Whether it is professionally, financially, spiritually or physically related, you are probably working on something to enhance your life and the lives of others. Whatever you're doing, hold on and keep trusting that great things will come to pass. Reject thoughts of complacency and dismiss the need to fear old statements that occasionally creep in your mind. Hold on and keep following your heart to accomplish what you're really meant to do.

For the last couple of weeks (mainly the last one), I should have reminded myself of the previous statements as my thoughts were disjointed and I felt very confused about what my future really holds. I read several affirmations and prayed more than usual to get myself back on track. But I was still frustrated. This was especially upsetting because I work daily to keep the right mindset and trust that no matter what happens in life everything works out for my good.

February 4, marking a month until my birthday, was a turning point for me. That evening after work, one of my dearest friends and I were talking while riding the train. She told me that I would overcome my challenging week. Shortly after she said that I broke out in tears and they flowed for a while. I stopped crying in time to exit the train and walk home. However, as soon as I was settled in the house, the tears flowed freely down my face again for several minutes. I eventually called my sister who encouraged me not to be ashamed of the tears because I was just moving to a new level of understanding. As I strove to focus only on positive thoughts and achieve my life's purpose, old ways of thinking and feelings of dealing with life as it is, tried to consume my mind. Before going to bed that night, I decided to think positively and keep working to fulfill my heart's desires.

Have you ever had a similar experience? I imagine that you already have or will in the future, and, trust me, you do get through these situations successfully when you do new things and let your inner self guide you.

Are you really fulfilled in all aspects of your life? If your answer is yes, that's wonderful and I hope you continue to follow your heart and do what's best for your life. If you answered no, hold on and take bold steps to push against mediocrity. Listen to your spirit and watch how the Creator directs you each day to do what you're really meant to do, be your true self; unite with the man or woman who is meant JUST for you, and beyond. We must hold on and move through the journey with ease!

Hold on!
Rebecca

My Insight

Spring

Love and Patience

Greetings!

We're in the midst of spring and there is evidence of growth everywhere. Green leaves are appearing on trees, flowers are budding, and people are entering and exiting our lives. Many people are also moving on from one opportunity to the next. Where are you in your life now?

Do you feel like you're not growing? Are you annoyed with the way your life is going? You're not alone. Recently, I've had conversations with individuals who have worked for a while at places they don't really like or they've been searching for new opportunities, to no avail. Situations like these cause many of us to get depressed, stressed, and upset. Yet we must remember that sometimes life's challenges are part of our growth. More importantly, we have the power to stay hopeful to win all battles.

I recently saw a blind man and his family on a bus. He sat holding a baby girl while his wife held another girl who appeared to be around four-years-old. I imagined how this man must have felt upon learning that he was blind. He was probably frustrated and afraid of the future. But those feelings weren't apparent when I saw him and his family. He was putting shoes on his baby daughter's feet and talking to his wife. When they prepared to get off the bus, the blind man helped his family exit the bus safely. Amazing! I thought that was one of the best examples of a person who has overcome difficulties. Certainly, we can all do great things, whether we're looking for a new job, overcoming the loss of loved ones, or trying to release the feeling of being annoyed because we work long hours day after day.

In essence, get excited about your future! You can overcome WHATEVER situation(s) currently face you. The new job or business deal you need is unfolding now. You're becoming healthier than ever before, so sickness is leaving your body right now. The precious loved one you lost is free of this world's troubles and his or her spirit will live forever. The bill you're stressing over is taken care of because the Universe is providing you with necessary money to pay it now.

Continue to focus on life's blessings regardless of life's storms. Remember, you'll always overcome with love and patience!

Going Forward with Love and Patience!
Rebecca

My Insight

Embrace Expressions of Love

Greetings!

Spring is finally here. It's a wonderful time to realize the blessings of love that are all around us. Expressions of love are everywhere, but everyday life sometimes makes us less aware of them. We should embrace love that is ever flowing and powerful.

This spring, I have become more conscious of love in my life and it has made my world much more peaceful and worthwhile. Have you experienced recently some of the following love expressions, as I have?

- A hug from a relative you had not seen in a long time.
- An e-mail confirming a business deal you hoped to acquire.
- Your song plays on the radio in the middle of traffic.
- A post on social media sent from an acquaintance who normally does not write you.
- Rubs on your back from a significant other after you hear less than favorable news.
- A telephone call from the one person who makes you smile gleefully.
- Holding hands with that special person who makes you feel beautiful, childlike and safe all at once.
- A colleague or student offers feedback, saying "You make everything make sense."
- A neighbor opens the door so you can walk to the laundry room without dropping your clothes bag.
- A baby coos and smiles at you.
- A toddler waves goodbye to you in the elevator.
- A loved one wakes up early to make your breakfast because you're in too much pain to do it yourself.
- A friend sends a text message offering to take you to dinner.
- A loved one provides a financial gift to you just because he or she cares.

- Multiple people send you greeting cards on your birthday.
- A friend stops by your house with a gift for your child.
- A loved one buys roses for you on the same day you bought a rose for yourself.
- Someone special sends a package of thoughtfully personalized items just for you, unexpectedly.
- A grocery store cashier shares his or her store membership number so you can get grocery savings.
- A new acquaintance applauds your efforts towards achieving your goals, and provides you with insight to help you move to the next level.
- Many loved ones attend your housewarming and express how proud they are to see how well you have grown.
- A person opens the train car door so for you to enter before him or her.

Points made on this list are great reminders of how much love may be flowing in your day-to-day life. Imagine how much more amazing and peaceful the world would be if everyone fully embraced such expressions of love? Oftentimes, people equate love with romantic feelings but it is much more than that. Our "common" life experiences are seasoned with love that should be appreciated daily. Remember to encourage others to nurture love regularly.

> Embracing Love and Blessings for All,
> Rebecca

My Insight

Summer

Love Conquers All

Greetings!

How is your summer going? I imagine that it has been filled with many blessings, such as: love, peace, health, and prosperity as well as joyful times with loved ones, new business deals, and relaxing moments by yourself. No matter what you have experienced this summer, I hope you have grown stronger and more committed to fulfill your amazing potential.

We are here on Earth working daily to stand tall and reach higher heights. While we work in a multitude of ways with a variety of people, we all essentially have the same needs. For example, a multimillionaire desires to provide a wonderful home and life for his or her family just as people who only have a few dollars want to do the same for their families. We should work together to enhance all lives despite how our circumstances differ. The Universe will allow us to conquer at any level. One of the wonderful things about the Universe is that it blesses us to improve the world and make our dreams come true. Unfortunately, we don't always follow through on our goals because we feel lost or doubtful about what's to come. We have to decide to trust our hearts and be excited about what's to come.

This summer, the truth screamed loudly at me as my corporate job ended in June. You're reading correctly; my job ended. It was bound to happen because I said I would only work there two years when I started (which I did). Additionally, I was frustrated and tired for the first half of this year. My heart continuously told me that there was much more to my life than working in a corporate office for ridiculously long hours. Now, I work hours doing what I enjoy and that will make a real difference in the lives of others.

Some people might think it's sad that I no longer have a corporate job, but I'm pleased to tell you that my life has improved greatly since June.

Since then, I have worked to:
- Develop relationships with small business owners to serve as their communications consultant;
- Give presentations and develop skills through a public speaking organization;
- Prepare to teach another year of enrichment courses every other Saturday through an organization;
- Propose and secure a contract with a new high school to teach Spanish and motivational classes;
- Develop a presentation for suburban school teachers based on my motivational lessons; and
- Write messages similar to this one to submit to inspirational magazines.

In addition to working on the above, I attended an excellent seminar where I learned new ways to build wealth. The seminar is a nice complement to books I have read in order to develop and implement my wealth plan. As a great friend recently said to me, "There is more money than air out here – get your share."

Don't you love that?! I hope you're working strategically to get your share and staying open to generosity from other sources. I hope you see that when life seems to unravel you have to say I'm going to make it! I say: "I'm going to make it BETTER THAN EVER." Remember that you can make it through anything because love conquers all. Just take time to be still, listen to the truth in your heart, and take action. Then, you'll quickly see how things unfold beautifully in your life.

> Conquering and Embracing Greater Success for All,
> Rebecca

My Insight

Turn Worry Into Wonderful

Greetings!

Are you enjoying the first part of July? I welcomed the month with open arms as I had moments of anxiety at the end of June. Maybe you felt similarly. I am pleased to remember and remind you that there are wonderful reasons why we must move beyond worry and fall in love with life again.

You may think that falling in love is about your relationships. That is not always true. Falling in love, or what I prefer to call taking an offer of new love, can include loving a new business, career, or class; loving a new hobby; loving a new home; or loving a new baby or pet in your family. While I had moments of anxiety about how my future would unfold, I was fortunate to break through the mental angst thanks to meditation and the examples of loved ones moving through life smoothly.

Recently, one couple I know got engaged, while another one had a healthy baby. Taking note of how my friends had new reasons for embracing life and love helped me remember that over-thinking and worrying about the future is unnecessary. Life may seem dark in our minds, but it only takes a slight change of mind to move us to the light.

Please join me in remembering regularly that our questions are answered in time or, I should say, the right time. Fretting continuously about every detail of the future is not worthwhile. Infinite Spirit is always inside you gladly providing the answers you need at the perfect moments.

I am recommitted to embracing each new day with confidence, love, passion, and purpose. My life and yours is unfolding nicely as long as we believe that there's always a reason for falling in love with life.

Stay present and love life,
Rebecca

My Insight

Moving

Greetings!

How is life treating you these days? Did your summer fly by quickly or pass slowly? Regardless of the speed of your life currently, it is safe to say that it is moving.

We are in constant motion and we have to press forward daily to fulfill our destinies. You may understand this concept in theory, but do you really embrace it each day? With technology and other societal advances developing rapidly, it serves us well to keep moving ahead. Just waking up every morning is reason to be excited about fulfilling your destiny.

Recently, I have enjoyed both rapid and slow movement in my life. I have experienced fast, wonderful changes physically and spiritually. Each day, I take more care regarding what I eat and drink, while ensuring that thoughts of love and divine health only reign in my mind as I enjoy my meals. In a short stint of time, both my body and spirit have become healthier and stronger than ever! I also have appreciated more deliberate movement in my business endeavors. I made a more aggressive push for Spanish classes and motivational presentation clients, and I now have a couple of serious inquiries for my Spanish service. In addition, one well-known educational organization is interested in my motivational training and a popular journalist is willing to provide me with more resources to get more trainings. No matter what, I keep it moving. Whether rapid or slow, I can attest to how being in constant motion will give you a great sense of joy and drive to fulfill your life's mission(s).

How many times have you felt that you cannot or do not want to move forward? I certainly have been there and I imagine that you have, too. This summer, I witnessed the power of turning to the Creator, as a family friend (we will call her Leslie) had four loved ones pass away in consecutive weeks. As you can probably imagine by reading this, my friend and her family were worn out! After the last funeral, Leslie, other loved ones, and I celebrated the lives of those who passed on as well as our own lives with music and laughter. Throughout the celebration and upon hearing news of prior transitions, Leslie focused on the One who motivates and strengthens. Thanks to that Guiding Light, she and her family keep it moving to brighter days.

Are you stuck in a rut because a loved one has passed away, or work is no longer fulfilling, or your relationship is not where you want it to be? As autumn moves full speed ahead, let the old leaves or old thoughts and ways of living blow firmly out of your mind FOR GOOD! In turn, fully embrace loving, positive thoughts in your mind this season and regularly. I know that I have, and am, doing so. And something tells me that amazing experiences are just around the corner. Remember, you always win when you stay focused on greatness and move!

Here's to living Happier, Lighter, and Mightier!
Rebecca

My Insight

Everything and More

Greetings, Wonderful!

Are you feeling that there is more to life than what you are currently experiencing? Do you know deep in the core of your being that there is more to life than just completing mundane tasks day after day? Are you often thinking, "I know I'm meant to be or to have more than this?"

I can say yes to all three of those questions and perhaps you can, too.

It is fantastic to know that while we question life at times, the Creator/Universe consistently provide for us. If we feel sometimes that there's nothing much to be grateful for or enjoy, we can simply look at the sun, the moon, the stars and nature in general for sweet reminders of the Universe's provision. Plus, we can feel very empowered and loved because the Creator wants the very best for us and loves us dearly. Ponder that for a minute. Don't you feel amazed to know about the Creator's relation to you? And when you ask yourself questions like: "Is there more to life than this?" Trust what comes to you and act on it.

During a recent trip, I met a woman who left her husband of ten years after he became abusive. She told me that she was initially scared to live alone after living with her husband for so long. Yet, God told her she was taken care of so bit by bit she became less fearful and stronger. Now she lives in a different city and state from her ex-husband, in a safe environment that she loves. What courage she demonstrated!

I have also been reminded by the Universe about expanding my life and expressing more greatness. While my Spanish instruction with youth is worthwhile, I have had promptings to do more writing and help people like you! Additionally, I keep receiving messages to be unlimited and to imagine living more abundantly. We all have the ability to imagine our lives as more expansive than what's generally known as necessary and part of what we're intended to do on Earth.

We have to know that the Creator has equipped us to be great and live very well. We can be blessed with everything and more. In other words, when we think we have asked, visualized, or prayed for everything, we can be blessed with even more than that! Take a few moments to think about "everything" that you had once, but at some point later you wanted more. And hopefully, you were able to experience more or get more to move farther along your life path.

What more is your soul calling for now? Do you really have courage and faith to ask for a new "everything and more?" We are really amazing expressions of the Creator so let's act like it by dreaming and acting boldly, asking questions about what we need to do, and trust wholeheartedly that our new "everything" and "more" will bring much joy and the satisfaction that we truly deserve.

> Much love and imagining everything and more for all!
> Rebecca

My Insight

End of Year

Golden Teardrops Bring Freedom

Greetings!

Can you believe that it's already December 2009, and we will soon enter the last year of the first decade of the 21st century? I hope you have made the most of this year. Like mine, I imagine that your past year has been full of both blessings and challenges. Thank God that lessons learned from our challenges help us grow into better people. Two of the greatest lessons I learned this year were to not waste time and to open my heart by letting go of past hurts.

Life's challenging circumstances can cause anyone to cry at times. But when we cry, eventually we must dry our eyes and move forward to live more purposefully, using our time wisely because we won't get it back.

I realized this firsthand earlier this year when I cried about not doing my life's work. Thankfully, the Creator helped me to dry my eyes and push forward to fulfill one of my life's missions to motivate people through music. This spring, I started with one motivational music class and have added two more classes since then. And, I was blessed with a large speaking engagement that included 120 adults and children. Everyone was thoroughly engaged during the session and I was even asked to speak at the school again. See what happens when you awaken to the Creator's truth and take greater control of your life? As I write this message, I know that more opportunities are unfolding for you and me. We don't have time to waste. We must take control and fulfill our heart's desires.

In addition to learning how to take more control of my life professionally, I've learned to completely release the past and open the door to my heart again. During the last couple of months, I had experiences that made me realize the need to fully release all thoughts of past hurts, especially in the area of romantic love and relationships.

My last romantic relationship ended five years ago and left me with wounds that I thought would have healed before now. However, that wasn't the case. My heart was completely open during that relationship, and I shut it tightly after it ended. While I dated within the past five years, subconsciously I would not get too close to a new acquaintance because I didn't want to be hurt again. Recently, I let all thoughts regarding my past relationship and love in general flow freely. As I asked for forgiveness of those feelings, I was freed: body, mind, and spirit. Now I feel freer than ever, with clear thoughts and the confidence that new love is on the horizon.

An important person in my life often tells me: "Remain free." So I ask you: Are you truly free of past business or job loss, a relationship gone sour, or doubts about yourself? Take time this month to COMPLETELY release unhappy thoughts about those occurrences and let wounds heal, so you can end the year with the sense of real freedom, joy, and peace that will spill over into more dynamic life experiences in 2010.

With an Open Heart,
Rebecca

My Insight

Growing Up

Sweet Greetings to you!

I hope you are very well and that your life experiences are unfolding wonderfully. As another year comes to a close, I'm reminded of the power of growing in both challenging and seamless processes. Let's look more into the importance of growing up.

Whether you feel this year was full of lows or countless highs, growth and learning took place that hopefully provided you with the wisdom to move forward with maturity. Life guides men and women towards maturity. I've learned that the sooner we heed direction from within our souls the better off we are, and the faster we move to higher levels of awareness. Specifically, wisdom from within encouraged me to take more time to meditate or be still daily so I can live more abundantly spiritually, physically, and financially. I was reminded to do so earlier in the year, but I fully followed that message at the beginning of this month. The end result is that I am happier and clearer about being grateful for what I am doing now, while staying open and trusting in greater life experiences to come.

Oftentimes, I am intrigued by expressions made by men in my life or by the men in the lives of people I know. Two similar thoughts seem to be shared by these men: one that he is not all that he should be; and, two, that he doesn't have the material things that he believes he should have at a particular point in his life. Now, I understand why a man, or a woman, might feel this way. BUT, I kindly ask every man reading this to consider why he may think this way. If your reasons are based on the opinions of others, then delete them from your mind and embrace the thought that you are great just because of whom you really are and you will keep growing to do better. Personally, I applaud men who are grateful for where they are, while knowing that greater life experiences and the very best of life will constantly come their way. They remain open to richer experiences, are connected to the Creator, take proper action, and are ever grateful.

Some men and women may say that growing up can be a painful. Note that it "can be," but it doesn't "have to be." Recently, I explained to loved ones that I wholeheartedly believe that we can grow up without enduring extreme challenges. For example, one day I moved too fast when parking and scratched my car window. I grew from that experience, and learned to take more time when parking while looking at all sides of the space before backing up. This would be a "growing up is painful" experience if I continued to move incorrectly into the parking space with the window breaking into pieces. I don't know about you, but I prefer the less challenging growth process. I certainly hope that your life is only filled with minimal challenges.

Whatever growing occurred in your life this year, embrace it and know that you have the power to keep holding on, growing, and being the best expression of the Creator that you are meant to be. Be confident and have faith that the next year and your next steps in life are directing you toward greatness.

>Much love and only the very best in all!
>Rebecca

My Insight

About the Author

Rebecca L. Chauncey is an in-demand professional speaker, writer, and workplace transformer who is often called a ray of sunshine. She wholeheartedly embraces excitement for everyday life, like dancing in her seat while eating delicious foods or singing thank you repeatedly after completing work. Rebecca also joyfully shares her "rays of sunshine" to help people live fully and share positivity in personal and professional settings. She has experienced professional success in academic, corporate, and governmental sectors. With her rich knowledge of diverse business fields and passion for experiencing the best of daily life, she clearly knows the importance of celebrating precious moments and overcoming challenges to succeed in life. Contact Rebecca about this book and for speaking engagements via LinkedIn or send an email to youcanstilllive@gmail.com.

Made in the USA
Charleston, SC
22 July 2016

CINCINNATI CEMETERIES

Hauntings and Other Legends

ROY HEIZER

Photography by Nancy Heizer

Schiffer Publishing Ltd
4880 Lower Valley Road • Atglen, PA 19310

Other Schiffer Books by the Author:

Haunted Charlotte: Supernatural Stories from the Queen City. ISBN: 978-0-7643-4703-0
Savannah's Garden Plants. ISBN: 978-0-7643-3265-4
Savannah's Historic Churches. ISBN: 978-0-7643-3864-9
Coastal Garden Plants: Maine to Maryland. ISBN: 978-0-7643-4402-2
Atlanta's Garden Plants. ISBN: 978-0-7643-3810-6
Coastal Garden Plants: Florida to Virginia. ISBN: 978-0-7643-4181-6

Other Schiffer Books on Related Subjects:

Cincinnati Ghosts. Karen Laven. ISBN: 978-0-7643-2899-2
Ohio's Haunted Crimes: An Exploration of Ten Haunted Crime Scenes. Kat Klockow. ISBN: 978-0-7643-5011-5
Strange Ohio Monsters. Michael Newton. ISBN: 978-0-7643-4397-1

Copyright © 2017 by Roy Heizer

Library of Congress Control Number: 2017936640

All rights reserved. No part of this work may be reproduced or used in any form or by any means—graphic, electronic, or mechanical, including photocopying or information storage and retrieval systems—without written permission from the publisher.

The scanning, uploading, and distribution of this book or any part thereof via the Internet or any other means without the permission of the publisher is illegal and punishable by law. Please purchase only authorized editions and do not participate in or encourage the electronic piracy of copyrighted materials.

"Schiffer," "Schiffer Publishing, Ltd.," and the pen and inkwell logo are registered trademarks of Schiffer Publishing, Ltd.

Type set in NewYorkerType/Times New Roman

ISBN: 978-0-7643-5316-1
Printed in China

Published by Schiffer Publishing, Ltd.
4880 Lower Valley Road
Atglen, PA 19310
Phone: (610) 593-1777; Fax: (610) 593-2002
E-mail: Info@schifferbooks.com
Web: www.schifferbooks.com

For our complete selection of fine books on this and related subjects, please visit our website at www.schifferbooks.com. You may also write for a free catalog.

Schiffer Publishing's titles are available at special discounts for bulk purchases for sales promotions or premiums. Special editions, including personalized covers, corporate imprints, and excerpts, can be created in large quantities for special needs. For more information, contact the publisher.

We are always looking for people to write books on new and related subjects. If you have an idea for a book, please contact us at proposals@schifferbooks.com.

DEAD-ICATION

These stories are "Dead-icated" to my father, Raymond T. Heizer, whose spirit haunts me every time I visit his grave in Highland Cemetery.

It is also dedicated to the many men and women who lost their lives during the Cincinnati-wide influenza outbreak of 1918–1919.

Contents

Acknowledgments. 6
Introduction. 7

1. Highland Cemetery / St. Mary's Cemetery:
   A Mysterious Burial in the Heizer Plot. 8
2. Glen Haven Cemetery: The Strange Life of Joseph C. Maller. 11
3. Highland Cemetery: Boo Ghost 14
4. Highland Cemetery: The Murder of Harvey Myers 16
5. Highland Cemetery / Kenton County Burial Grounds:
   Where the Unknown Wander 19
6. Linden Grove Cemetery: Covington Carl. 22
7. Linden Grove Cemetery: The Guard of Linden Grove. 29
8. Oak Hill Cemetery: The Weird Guy 32
9. Spring Grove Cemetery: John R. Hugh 43
10. Spring Grove Cemetery:
    The Gate—That Which Enters Never Leaves. 46
11. Spring Grove Cemetery: Paranormal Investigation 49
12. St. John German Catholic Cemetery: An Unsettled Haunting 61
13. St. John German Catholic Cemetery: Caparra 65
14. St. Mary's Graveyard (Cincinnati): The Fleague 77
15. St. Mary's Graveyard (Cincinnati):
    A Sense of Immeasurable Sorrow. 80
16. St. Mary's Graveyard (Cincinnati):
    What's Haunting St. Mary's Graveyard? 84
17. St. Mary's Cemetery (Ft. Mitchell, Kentucky):
    A Well-Dressed Ghost. 88
18. Vine Street Hill Cemetery: Dr. Aljuzza. 92
19. Walnut Hills Cemetery: Ghost in the Fireplace 96
20. Walnut Hills Cemetery: Till Death Do Us Rest 100
21. Walnut Hills Cemetery: A Haunted History 105
22. Cincinnati Cemeteries:
    Weeping Willows and Other Graveyard Symbology 107

Conclusion 111

Acknowledgments

The author wishes to acknowledge the people, living and dead, of Cincinnati, especially those working for or with these hauntingly beautiful burial grounds.

I also wish to thank my sister, Joanne D. Heizer Hetzel, for her help with the Heizer family genealogy.

I want to acknowledge Anders Manga and Devallia Anders for creating some of the most inspiring, Gothic and haunting music . . . to which to write a book of ghost stories.

INTRODUCTION

Welcome to some of the strangest stories ever disinterred about the burial grounds of greater Cincinnati. From a mysterious burial to "The Fleague," *Cincinnati Cemeteries* offers insight into the paranormal realm beyond the eternal curtain. Legends and fables tell of oddities and apparitions that roam among the sleeping.

From The Laboytraux-Cary Cemetery to the Clifton Jewish Cemetery, and many others, Cincinnati cemeteries offer bucolic views, a rich history, and some very weird tales from beyond the grave. Be brave, or be afraid . . .

The Clifton Jewish Cemetery. Have you heard the enthralling legend of how this Jewish burial ground came into existence?

CHAPTER ONE

Highland Cemetery
St. Mary's Cemetery

A Mysterious Burial in the Heizer Plot

The Heizer family plot—the site of an unauthorized burial that remains a family mystery to this day.

In 1995, my father, Raymond Heizer, Jr., went to Highland Cemetery to arrange for his burial next to his father, Raymond Heizer, Sr., in the Heizer family plot. What he was told began a family mystery that has now become a mysterious legend at the cemetery.

He was told that there was already someone else buried in that grave. There was no headstone, and my father knew not of such an interment. My father was not one to let such things go unnoticed. No relative of his had died recently. A mystery of grave proportions was about to be unearthed . . . or was it? So who was it that was buried in his grave? Who authorized the burial, and why? A strange mystery indeed!

Highland Cemetery records indicated that it was Florence Slater Pierce, who had been buried there on July 18, 1981, some fourteen years prior. She had died on June 11, 1981, in Terrace Park, Ohio. The question of *who?* was answered, but the question of *by whom and why?* remained a mystery.

At the time, my father had proprietorship over the family plot, and any burial would have needed his approval, but he had not authorized her interment. There was no record of who authorized the burial of Florence Slater Pierce in his plot. He inquired with his two sisters, (my aunts) Virginia Hickenlooper and Betty Powell, but they knew nothing of the mysterious burial either.

My father was something of a Spiritualist, an amateur medium, so he attempted to contact the spirit of Florence Pierce and ask her who had buried her there and why. All attempts to reach her failed. It seemed she had literally taken her secrets to the grave. Now you know where the saying "dead men tell no tales" comes from.

My father, not one to let a mystery go unsolved, pursued an answer to his questions until his own death on March 30, 1996. He was buried at Highland Cemetery in the Heizer plot, but on the other end of the burial row from his father. I attended his graveside service there on a chilly day in early April, as a few snowflakes floated down from a lugubrious sky.

My older sister, Joanne, continued the search for answers. She did some genealogy and inquired further with family and the available records. Her research took her to the end of the paperwork's trail. The following is what she was able to piece together of the mysterious interment. (We all know that paperwork does not always tell the whole story. It is only an educated guess as to what really happened . . .)

Through family genealogy, she found out that Florence Slater Pierce's sister, Lucille Slater Heizer, was the widow of Joseph B. Heizer Jr. Joseph was the brother of our grandfather Raymond T. Heizer Sr., making him our great uncle and Lucille Slater Heizer our great aunt. That would make Florence Slater Pierce, the woman at the heart of the mystery, our great aunt once removed. She was, after all, a somewhat distant relative. Cemetery records list Lucille Slater Heizer

St. Mary's Graveyard, adjacent to Highland Cemetery, contains the only suspect in a strange family mystery.

as the next of kin and our best guess as to who authorized the burial, although we do not know this for sure. The question of why remained.

It turned out that Joseph B. Heizer Jr. died and was buried in the Heizer plot in 1953, and it would have been expected that Lucille Slater Heizer would have been buried with him. But she was Catholic and would have wanted to be buried with her family next door at St. Mary's Catholic Cemetery. This would have left her spot available. In the time between Joseph B. Heizer's death and her death, both our grandparents, Raymond T. Heizer Sr. and his wife, Elizabeth Heizer, died and were buried in the Heizer plot, separating the graves of Joseph and Lucille Heizer. We think that Florence Slater Pierce was no longer Catholic and, therefore, could not be buried in St. Mary's Cemetery, and so her sister had her buried in Highland, in her space, so they could be near each other. Lucille apparently thought that the space at Highland was hers to use as she saw fit, most likely not knowing that she needed authorization.

When Lucille Slater Heizer died on February 23, 1982, she was buried in section 9-B, lot #246, in St. Mary's Catholic Cemetery next to Highland Cemetery.

In more recent years, various family members have offered other explanations for the unauthorized burial of Florence Slater Pierce in the Heizer family plot. Those explanations range from a dispute with Lucille Heizer over a farm to the ghost of Joseph B. Heizer Jr., who still haunts the plot to this day. He is said to still be looking for his missing wife.

The mystery of the unauthorized burial remains just that, a mystery. We are only guessing as to what really happened and why. We will most likely never know the whole story. The truth . . . well . . . who's to say?

CHAPTER TWO

Glen Haven Cemetery

The Strange Life of Joseph C. Maller

Police evidence photo of Joseph C. Maller's mangled remains.

Perhaps it was the fact that he was born at the onset of the Civil War. Perhaps it was the turbulent times in which he was brought into this world. Perhaps it was just fate. But right from the start Joseph C. Maller was a peculiar case. The midwife at his birth thought that he had some strange magical powers, while others thought that he was going to be a nefarious adult. Whatever it was, he had an aura about him.

He was born just as the Civil War was getting underway, on the hot and humid day of August 18, 1860, in Hamilton County, Ohio, to parents unnamed. Only four pieces of paperwork and a small footstone are all that is known about Joseph C. Maller. The first is a letter written by his mother that includes details of his birth. The second is a journal kept by one of his grade-school teachers. The third is a criminal record write-up at the Hamilton County Courthouse dated Monday, September 19, 1887. The last is a newspaper article dated December 9, 1889.

His mother's letter indicated she shared the midwife's concern that something was odd about the infant Joey. The letter rambled on for quite some time about her "interestingly different" baby boy.

It seems that during the 1873–1874 school year Mrs. Smith, one of the local teachers, had a most "preoccupied" student by the name of Joey Maller, according to her journal entries for that school year. She noted that he had been born at the new city hospital, and that her sister Ellen was one of the nurses in charge of his care.

Her first entry about Joey was her concern that he was not getting along with the other students. He seemed distant and unwilling to participate in the normal activities that the other children enjoyed. The entry called him "a fractious young man." The second entry about Joey Maller was to share her concern that he was preoccupied with the killing of big and small game near the schoolhouse. There were rumors that he had sacrificed the animals in some sort of attempt to see if they had spirits that would rise up out of their bodies at the time of death. While the other boys were known to practice hunting squirrels and rats, Joey was caught shooting at the neighborhood chickens and livestock. She also noted that the other children were lodging complaints to their parents and teachers of bullying and "the employment of black magic." A third entry, dated March 1874, stated that Joey was on the verge of being kicked out of school for his "bizarre and disruptive" behavior. Mrs. Smith made her last, perhaps ominous, entry about Joey Maller on April 2, 1874, when she stated that she felt he was, despite everyone's efforts to help the young man, forever lost.

There is no record of Joseph C. Maller between the summer of 1874 and September 1887, a span of thirteen years. These formative years of his life remain a mystery open to guessing and speculation.

Joseph C. Maller did re-emerge in the public record on September 19, 1887 when he turned up in a criminal complaint filed by the Hamilton County Police

Department. The complaint alleged that one Joseph C. Maller, whose occupation was listed as gravedigger, was sought in the killing of an award-winning show dog, an Airedale owned by Mr. and Mrs. Thomas N. Bouchant. The Airedale, Curly, was estimated to be worth over $400 due to winnings and endorsements.

According to the complaint, Joseph Maller and the Bouchants were both strolling, separately, through the Glen Haven Cemetery on the morning of September 17. Maller stopped the Bouchants so he could pet Curly and ask about the dog, whereupon he was told of Curly's status and worth. He petted Curly for several more minutes while chatting pleasantly with the Bouchants. Joe then strolled away from the Bouchants, and they moved off in the other direction. Maller then, according to the complaint, turned back towards the dog, took out a pistol and proceeded to shoot Curly twice in the head, killing him instantly. The Bouchants were shocked and horrified at the atrocity committed in front of them. Joseph C. Maller then slowly wandered off across the cemetery grounds. Two days later the Bouchants filed the criminal complaint against him.

The killing of a dog in those days was not a criminal offence, and the complaint was dropped over the objections of the Bouchants. They sought counsel from a lawyer over the matter. They were told that he might be in legal trouble for the discharge of a firearm in a public place, but that there was now no proof that the dog was shot by him, as there were no other witnesses. Besides, the lawyer stated, getting a conviction would be a long shot at best. So the lawyer eventually dissuaded them from filing a lawsuit. Legally the matter was over. But legally over and concluded are often two separate matters.

Just over two years later, in December of 1889, Joseph C. Maller's mangled body was found along one of the paths in the Glen Haven Cemetery, where he had been employed. He had apparently been mauled to death by a large dog. When he was found he had virtually no blood left in his body. What was left of his skin was the pale gray color of death. Maller had, according to witnesses, over four dozen bite marks and an uncountable number of claw scratches on his person. Witnesses to the carnage stated that his eyes were transfixed wide open, with dilated pupils . . . as if he'd had the fear of the devil in him when he was killed.

Many people in the years after told of seeing a large ghostly Airedale, presumably Curly, wandering proudly around the Glen Haven Cemetery. Witnesses say that while the dog is a ghostly pale figure, bright red blood drips profusely from his mouth, and his paws leave bloody prints behind momentarily wherever he strolls in the cemetery.

CHAPTER THREE

Highland Cemetery

Boo Ghost

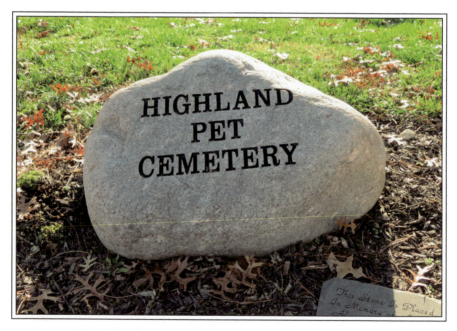

A mysterious feline is known to haunt Highland Pet Cemetery.

Highland Cemetery sits on 250 acres of rolling land in Ft. Mitchell, Kentucky, just south of Cincinnati proper. It has over 47,000 burials, but not all of them are human. Highland Cemetery also has a burial section for man's best friend, or any other family pet.

While it is well known that all dogs go to heaven, some cats have other fates. Fickle beasts in the best of times, cats are thought to have supernatural associations and magical powers. Cultures across time and geography have appreciated the mystical allure of cats, with their aloof and intelligent manners.

Boo, a solid black cat with large glowing eyes, was born on Halloween night 1990. He was named Boo because he was a Halloween kitten. Since his birth, Boo had always had a mysterious aura about him. He seemed to live in the shadows of his house and in the shadow of his owners' minds. His people, themselves a bit mysterious, claimed he was from another realm. For his many years, he cast a supernatural demeanor. Those that came across his path relayed some strange stories about Boo.

One such story began innocently enough at a dinner party in January or February 2003. The guests were all seated around the table about to indulge in the feast. John Transum, the host of the party and one of Boo's people, was pointing out all of the delicacies on display for the meal. Boo sat silently on the sideboard table watching the whole affair. John pointed out the small meat wraps neatly placed on a hand-painted blue plate near Tom Wajidawa. He pointed out several other items and gave a quick history on why they were included in the meal. Then he said: "Let's eat."

A few minutes later, Marcel Boumichauxi, the other host and John's partner, asked where the meat wraps had gone. The question went around the table with everyone denying that they had taken any of them. Even the plate was gone. John searched for it, but it had simply vanished. Balbo Weda gasped aloud, and everyone turned to see what he was gasping at; there sat Boo on the side table licking his lips. He at last looked up at the group staring at him and winked. The men all asked each other if anyone had seen Boo move across the table. They each answered "no." And yet, somehow, Boo had made himself invisible, slunk across the room, and taken the meat wraps . . . or had he?

Two weeks later, John found the blue plate in a trunk in the attic—the attic that only he and Boo ever entered. It was the same trunk where he stored what was to be his funeral suit.

The dinner party story was not the last odd story that has been associated with Boo. Over his many years, Boo was suspected in a number of fantastic stories that verged on the world of the unknown. There was the time Marcel watched Boo transmute from a cat into a dog right in front of him. Marcel swore off wine the next morning and has been sober ever since. Boo's ability to weave in and out of the shadows of the night seemed extraordinary, even for a cat.

Upon his earthly death in 2009, his owners had him buried in the pet section of Highland Cemetery. After that, both John and Marcel, as well as many other people, have claimed that the four-legged ghost of Boo still roams slyly under the moonlit nights through the cemetery, swirling through its ghostly shadows.

CHAPTER FOUR

Highland Cemetery

The Murder of Harvey Myers

One of Covington's most famous murder victims, attorney Harvey Myers, is interred in Highland Cemetery. His ghost can still be seen pacing there, as if he is still arguing before some supernatural judge.

Harvey Myers was born on February 10, 1828, in Chenango County, New York, to Aaron and Aurelia B. Myers. Through hard work and studious education, he received his degree and relocated to Covington, Kentucky, to teach school in 1851. He began work at a law office in 1853 and passed the Kentucky bar in 1854.

In the meantime he courted and married. His marriage produced six children, all of whom lived to adulthood.

By 1860, he had formed a law partnership with the Honorable John W. Stevenson. Stevenson had just been elected governor of Kentucky and later went on to become a United States senator. The practice at Stevenson & Myers was busy, and the firm became quite successful in those years. Though he was a full-time lawyer, Mr. Myers found time to research and published the first "Code of Practice" for the commonwealth of Kentucky. It was known as "Myers' Code" and is still utilized by the Kentucky Bar Association. He compiled and published, in 1867, an auxiliary supplement to the General Statutes of Kentucky known as "Myers' Supplement to the General Statutes for the Commonwealth of Kentucky."

In 1865, Harvey Myers entered Kentucky politics as a Republican, being elected by the Union party to a post in the legislature. But there was a minor scandal involving the election proceedings, and Myers's ethics were brought into question. It seemed that bayonet-wielding soldiers were arresting the polling guards and turning away certain voters. The next day, Myers made a public proclamation that he would not have condoned such tactics and that he repudiated them. He then declined the office, saying that if he took the oath, some would see it as an endorsement of the tactics used by the soldiers. No one ever discovered who ordered the soldiers to act in such a manner.

Otherwise, Harvey Myers was revered among his colleagues and the citizens of Covington. The firm continued to attract clients and successfully dispose of case after case.

In the early 1870s, a local military officer by the name of Colonel William G. Terrell was involved in a turbulent marriage to a young woman. Terrell was well-known around town as a bully and a brute, having gotten into several scrapes with other local men. On two occasions he was jailed for assault. This aggressive personality brought him into direct conflict with his wife, who eventually filed for divorce. She sought counsel from Harvey Myers.

The young woman came in to Stevenson & Myers to give her deposition. She told Myers, on the record, of the abuse she had suffered at the hands of her husband. She stated that she needed a divorce for her protection.

Soon, though, word of the deposition's contents and accusations got back to Colonel Terrell, and he vowed to get revenge. His wife was placed in a safe house.

On the morning of March 28, 1874, Colonel William G. Terrell forced his way into the law office of Harvey Myers. The two men, according to witnesses, exchanged words. Terrell using "the foulest of language the devil himself would have been ashamed to use," one witness was quoted as saying.

Myers eventually demanded that Terrell leave his office, but Terrell refused to do so, leading to a physical confrontation between the men. It was at this time that Terrell pulled out a pistol and shot Myers in the abdomen. Myers staggered backwards, fell limply to the floor, and bled out. He was pronounced dead just over twenty minutes later.

Terrell was arrested and, after a lengthy and onerous trial, was convicted of second-degree murder. A divorce decree was immediately granted to his wife, so that she could find another means of support. Court documents related to his sentence are mysteriously missing, but it can be presumed that he was executed by hanging, for that was the typical punishment for that crime at that time. As with many convicts who were executed in those days, he would have been buried in an unmarked grave to be forgotten by the world.

The body of Harvey Myers was laid to rest in Highland Cemetery. The funeral was attended by many high-ranking officials, as well as his widow and children. His ghost is known to haunt the cemetery, having been seen on several occasions walking back and forth waving his right index finger in the air, as if he were giving evidence before the court.

CHAPTER FIVE

HIGHLAND CEMETERY
KENTON COUNTY BURIAL GROUNDS

Where the Unknown Wander

Kenton County Burial Grounds, where the unknown wander.

Alongside Highland Cemetery sits the old Kenton County Burial Grounds. This graveyard was originally designated as the African-American section before burial grounds were integrated. It also served as the anonymous section, a place to bury those who were unidentified or abandoned to the county because the family was too poor to afford a proper grave and headstone. The old Kenton County Burial Grounds, perhaps due to circumstances in which an unidentified person would have had to have died, are known to be haunted by several ghosts. These spirits, disconnected from both life and death, wander around the grounds. lost for eternity. While the rest of Highland Cemetery has its stories and legends, the old Kenton County Burial Grounds are considered the most haunted section. Even though the site looks like an empty field due to a lack of headstones, there are actually several dozen burials in the Kenton County Burial Grounds; among them, a most mysterious case . . .

In the early years of the twentieth century, northern Kentucky was a peaceful, bucolic place to call home. The Great War was over, industry was thriving; ships of all kinds moved goods, as well as people, up and down the Ohio River nearby. Shops were opening and the church pews were filled each Sunday. Greater Cincinnati was booming, and so was Covington. The town of Covington sits just across the Ohio River from Cincinnati, and serves as its largest bedroom community. In the early 1900s, Covington was sprucing up its public areas, building roads and designating parks for public use. One such reserve was Devou Park, a sprawling tract of land not far from downtown Covington. The residents of Covington knew Devou Park as a family-friendly place to have a picnic or take a stroll through the woods. A welcoming place . . . until 1924.

In the spring of 1924, the lifeless body of a young woman was found among the trees. A group of hikers found the rapidly decomposing remains just off one of the trails. She had been shot to death by an unknown assailant.

The police were called in to investigate. The body appeared as if it had been there several days, and any trace evidence was lost to time and weather. The body was taken to the local morgue for identification and a post-mortem. No identification was found with the body, and no identifying marks were found on it. She was photographed and her picture was put in the local paper, but no one came forward to identify her. Authorities were never able to establish her identity; in fact, most suspected she was not local. The post-mortem was able only to reaffirm the obvious: that she died of gunshot wounds to her chest and abdomen. The bullets were homemade, and a ballistics match was impossible. Her killer was never caught—for this crime, at least. A young woman in her late teens or early twenties, she died alone under violent and mysterious circumstances. She will never know justice. She was laid to rest in an unmarked grave in the old Kenton County Burial Grounds. Without a name, her burial was recorded in the records as unidentified.

Most ghost seekers agree that the ghosts of those who died suddenly and violently are the most likely to leave their spiritual residue behind their mortal lives. It is as if their soul, or spirit, within continues unaware of what has happened to their physical bodies. "A spirit in motion tends to stay in motion" might be a good way of describing why people who are murdered most often tend to be found in the ghostly realm. As for the young lady murdered in Devou Park . . . her ghost still haunts the grounds to this day. Several visitors have reported seeing a woman, dressed in 1920s clothing, approach them and then vanish . . . into the surreal void.

CHAPTER SIX

Linden Grove Cemetery

Covington Carl

The legendary graves of Mr. and Mrs. Steinforth. A local folk figure known as "Covington Carl" fell into infamy at this gravesite in Linden Grove Cemetery.

Everyone knew Carl Spencer as "Covington Carl," the town drunk. The local cops had hauled him to the drunk tank to sleep it off more times than they could count. He was generally regarded as harmless, even jovial, when in a state of intoxication. It was known around Covington that Carl would occasionally beg or try to scam someone out of a few dollars now and again. His actions were considered "petty" at best; his shenanigans were seen as more amusing than dangerous. As Carl was not considered a real criminal threat, most of the time, the locals just let him alone. It was not unusual for Carl to go missing for a couple of days at a time. "Oh, that Covington Carl; he's off on another toot," the neighbors would joke to themselves. Portly, slightly unkempt, and gregarious, Carl was somewhat of a local folk figure.

It was on a Tuesday in late January that old Mrs. Steinforth passed away. She had been for a few months the widow of George Steinforth, a prominent local businessman and major employer in the area. Mr. Steinforth had a reputation around town as a somewhat mysterious man, not prone to the usual fan-fare that many of his contemporaries displayed. He was known to have an iron fist and a subtle demeanor. Mrs. Steinforth dutifully played her role as his doting wife. She kept the parlor pristine and the bar stocked for the occasional businessman who might arrive without notice. The parlor, straight out of the Victorian era, was a large room framed by floor-length curtains and a finely made hand-carved bar.

In the mid-afternoon of the next day, gravediggers at the Linden Grove Cemetery, Henry and Daniel, received notification of her death. They knew that a ferocious snowstorm was on its way, and that if they didn't get started on her burial, they might not see the ground again until spring. They gathered up their picks and shovels and headed out to the Steinforth family plot in a race against the clock. The sun was beginning to set, and the temperatures were dropping fast. They arrived at the plot just as dark storm clouds were beginning to slowly roll in over the winter sky. Henry and Daniel were efficient at their jobs, and they had the grave open in just over an hour. The sun was just beginning to kiss the western horizon.

Later that evening, Carl slushed his way out of the Garrard Street Bar and began to stagger his way towards his run-down, low-rent home. He was headed to his house, but somewhere along the way he got turned around and started to wander into the Linden Grove Cemetery. The wind had picked up, and a few scattered snowflakes at the edge of the storm, reflecting off the street lamps, had begun to swirl around. He stumbled a little further into the graveyard before he noticed that he was going in the wrong direction to get home. As Carl was quite intoxicated, the snowflakes were not the only things swirling around his head. He stumbled onward in his usual awkward gait. His loud belching echoed off the surrounding gravestones. Meanwhile, down the street, someone yelled, "Shut up, Carl."

Suddenly, out of the darkness of the night, Carl began to hear a voice calling out from beyond the grave. He could not make out what the voice was saying, only that it was calling out to him. Carl was quite used to hearing voices while in an inebriated state, but this time the voice was different. What a mournful cry! In a panic, Carl looked around but saw only a cold, empty graveyard. He could see no one else. The voice echoed in Carl's head, but he could not tell where it was coming from. Was it in front of him, beckoning him onward, or did it come from behind, following him? The voice began to mingle with the alcohol, and Carl became frantic. His usual demeanor changed to consternation. He began to run in a state of heightened paranoia. Sweat rolled down over his rotund cheeks, and he tripped over several gravestones as he staggered among the old trees.

. . . And then, just as suddenly as the voice had come upon him, he felt the familiar sensation of falling—not, though, the feeling of tripping, which as a drunk he had experienced many times before, but rather the sensation that the ground was just no longer there. In a flash, drunk though he was, Carl realized that he was falling into an open hole in the ground. A large hole. A grave . . . a freshly dug grave. He crashed against the floor of the grave with a thud that surely would have awoken the dead. No sooner had he shaken the fall from his head than he once again heard the voice—the voice that had driven him to where he now was. But the voice was different this time; it didn't seem to be some far-off echo in the darkness, but came from right there in front of him. Carl waited for his eyes to adjust to the darkness, hoping to see where, or from whom, the sound was truly coming. His blurry vision was about to betray him.

The grave was particularly deep. Mrs. Steinforth had requested that it be seven feet deep, one more foot than the usual six. She had said the number seven was her lucky number, and she wanted to be buried at that depth. While the surrounding graveyard had been dark enough under the stormy night sky, the interior of the grave was a truly haunting darkness. His eyes eventually became as adjusted to the darkness as they were going to get. Carl again listened for the voice . . . but the grave was silent. All Carl could hear was a crow cackling off in the distance. A terrifying feeling came over him, and he swore right then and there that if he ever got out of this alive he'd never touch another drop of alcohol. The eerie tension was only heightened when Carl began to sense that perhaps he was not alone. Had some ghost come to visit him? Was a restless spirit resentful at his trespassing in its home? Were all his fears finally descending upon him at last? Was the voice going to return? The silence brought only a momentary reprieve from his terror.

But just as Carl's heart began to slow, he felt the most terrifying sensation of all . . . a hand upon his arm! He looked down only to see a bone-pale hand with translucent skeletal digits grasped tight around his forearm! Alcohol was no match for the state of mind he now found himself in.

Carl let out a scream that shattered the stillness of the night like a gunshot in a quiet forest; then things went black. When he came to consciousness, he opened his eyes only to be met with a long thin pallid face staring down at him. Through the diaphanous face, though, he could see the city lights reflecting off the clouds in the sky above the grave. He was face to form with the ghost of Mr. Steinforth, from the next grave over. Carl recognized the ghostly figure, and he instantly knew where he was. Carl pulled himself up just enough to squat. There before him was the ghostly spirit of a man he had known in life, but only from beyond the invisible walls of society's social curtain. Carl shivered in fear at the sight of Steinforth's ghost. At long last he asked the ghost, "The voice . . . the voice I heard that drove me here . . . was it yours?" In a seething voice the ghost replied, "Yes, and I have beckoned you here to exact my revenge upon you for how you wronged me. While others may have been entertained by your trickery, you cost me everything that was dear to me, and my wife her life . . . and you shall spend eternity smothered under the weight of my revenge."

Carl passed out again. The snowstorm at last came upon the grave, and by the time it passed, Covington Carl's frozen body was covered in several inches of snow at the bottom of the pit.

The next afternoon, after the graveside service, Mrs. Steinforth's coffin was lowered into the snow-filled grave, pushing Carl's frozen corpse down into the soft muddy dirt beneath it. Once the final prayers were said and the attendees had left, Henry and Daniel backfilled the grave as usual. They laid flowers on top to decorate the ground until the grass could grow over it later in the spring.

For the next several days, the Linden Grove Cemetery seemed quiet and peaceful. A couple of weeks later, someone finally asked, "Where is Covington Carl?" The question happened to be posed by someone sitting at the lunch counter of the local diner.

A police officer who was also sitting at the counter echoed the question, "Yeah, where *is* Carl?" After some inquiries were made around town, the policeman filed a missing person report. No one thought it was out of the question that Covington Carl had died in some obscure place while trying to get out of the cold of a northern Kentucky winter. Perhaps he had left town on the railway like so many hobos had done before. If only for the paperwork, the police in Covington needed an explanation, or a body.

A thorough search was conducted around town. The police and a small crew of volunteers searched through every alley and every flour barrel, through every attic and every root cellar. No human body was discovered.

In the meantime, the Steinforth estate was being reviewed by lawyers. The will left behind by Mrs. Steinforth was being challenged by one of the Steinforth children.

Covington Carl's watering hole, where this frighteningly funny tale began, was located on Garrard Street in downtown Covington.

The lawyers were alarmed that in the will and the corresponding paperwork there seemed to be a strong implication that Mrs. Steinforth thought she was about to be murdered . . . by one of her own children. It seemed that Mrs. Steinforth thought that her child, identified only as "C," had been slowly poisoning her. She had been sick for several months prior to her death, and she, according to her diary, suspected arsenic. The case was made all the more complicated by the fact that she had two sons, the elder, Charles, as well as Christopher, who were challenging the will. Both men were under suspicion.

The Steinforth paperwork seemed to be a rat's tunnel of implications, assumptions, and dead ends. The team of lawyers pored over what must have seemed like volumes of pages, all of them suggesting the mysterious "C" was feeding poison to Mrs. Steinforth. At long last the coroner who had signed her death certificate was questioned. He noted the cause of death as "Nondescript illness, aggravated by age." When questioned by police, he indicated that while something about her corpse didn't seem right, he had no reason to suspect foul play.

He would, though, at the police department's request, sign a certificate of exhumation. The coroner had always viewed himself as a competent man, and inquiry was part of the job. A second post-mortem was ordered, and Henry and Daniel braved the cold to exhume the body of Mrs. Steinforth. While several town officials looked on, the last of the ropes was tied around the coffin, and several men lifted it up out of the nearly frozen ground. One of the men remarked that the coffin seemed to weigh more than usual. The casket was more than halfway up when, surprisingly, it seemed to tilt. The men holding the ropes gripped tighter and pulled harder . . . then all of a sudden . . . the frozen corpse of Covington Carl dislodged itself from the underside of the coffin and crashed back down into the grave! The sudden change in weight took the rope pullers by surprise, and the coffin was flung like a rock in a slingshot onto the freshly dug pile of soil beside the open grave. It landed with a fierce thud, so hard that it popped open upon impact, and Mrs. Steinforth's body lay draped over the side. The unsightly scene was both horrifying and amusing.

Four Covington officials and two policemen peered over the edges of the open grave, only to see Carl's contorted corpse lying at the bottom. Both bodies were immediately taken to the city morgue. The police were glad they had found Carl's body. They learned the next morning that Henry and Daniel had opened the grave the afternoon prior to Mrs. Steinforth's being interred and they quickly surmised what had happened to him. That case, at least, was resolved.

A follow-up post-mortem was immediately conducted on Mrs. Steinforth. Her body was tested for a variety of commonly used poisons. Arsenic was one of the first poisons that the coroner tested for, and although her fingernails looked relatively normal, she did indeed have elevated levels of the toxin in her body. To rule out groundwater as a possible source, several other recently deceased persons were tested as well. Their results came back normal. It was only Mrs. Steinforth who had elevated arsenic levels in her system, leading to only one conclusion . . . murder!

There were only two remaining questions, "Who did it and why?"

The second question was pretty easy to figure out. The Steinforths were quite wealthy. With their mother out of the way, one of the two Steinforth boys would stand to inherit a very large sum of money, as well as extensive properties. The first question proved to be the more difficult one. The investigation quickly turned from "Who did it?" to "Which one did it?"

The first line of investigation centered on Charles, the eldest son, and the one who would, by being the eldest, be most likely to receive the lion's share of the inheritance. Why would, after all, Christopher kill his mother to then have to sue to get a decent share? Why not just kill his brother as well, and inherit everything? The next two days were a mad dash of inquiry, but all the clues came to dead ends. The police could not conclusively tie either son to the death of his mother. Suspicions and doubts were all the police had. Each piece of evidence contradicted another.

Meanwhile, the coroner's assistant began to prepare the corpse of Covington Carl for a proper pauper's burial in the general section of the Linden Grove Cemetery. When . . . all of a sudden . . . a letter fell out of his coat pocket. An old letter that appeared as if it had been in Carl's pocket for some time. A letter addressed to Mr. Steinforth of all people. When the assistant coroner opened the letter he was stunned to read what Carl had written in his own handwriting.

Mr. Steinforth,

I do so kindly thank you for your first three payments as per our agreement, but sir, we did agree to a payment of $250.00 a month for the rest of my life, and you have not made a payment for over two months now. I'm a patient man, but unless you want everyone in town to know that I am your true eldest son, and that you killed my unwed mother to conceal my birth, I suggest in the strongest of terms that I receive my next payment properly. You can consider yourself lucky that I care not about your wife or that you are poisoning her for discovering your secret. I care not about her, but I know your secrets, and I will never again live in a squalid house paying rent to you for a house that should rightfully be mine. Pay now, otherwise your family name will be ruined and your wedlock boys, my half-brothers, will be as penniless as you made me.

Yours truly,
Carl

Upon further inquiry, the letter found in Carl Spencer's pocket was accurate and truthful on all accounts. Carl's birth mother's grave was located in the paupers' section, disinterred, and examined. It was found to be filled with arsenic in the same quantities as Mrs. Steinforth's had been. The inquiry also exposed several love letters between Mr. and Mrs. Steinforth, leading to the revelation that Mr. Steinforth's middle name was Columbus, and that Mrs. Steinforth privately referred to him as "C" for short, not a reference to her children. Mr. Steinforth, it turned out, was a philanderer, a cheapskate, and a murderer!

Charles and Christopher were each awarded half of the remaining Steinforth estate. Charles took mostly liquid cash and rebuilt the family businesses to great success, while Christopher took the properties, made the necessary repairs, and became a successful and humane landlord. Perhaps Covington Carl was legally guilty of blackmail, but given the facts of the case and how his father had treated him for all those years, no one thought of him in any ill manner. The case was closed, but the ghost of Mr. Steinforth still haunts The Linden Grove Cemetery.

CHAPTER SEVEN

Linden Grove Cemetery

The Guard of Linden Grove

The gate to Linden Grove Cemetery is guarded by a ghostly figure who keeps watch over all those who are interred here.

The headstone of Charles Bennett, known locally as "the Guard of Linden Grove." According to local legend, he watches over those sleeping beyond the gate.

Linden Grove Cemetery sits on a hill overlooking Covington, Kentucky, in the shadow of Cincinnati. Since its first interment in 1843, this bucolic graveyard was Covington's most prestigious African-American burial ground. Originally known as the Cincinnati and Covington Cemetery, the leading figures of northern Kentucky's African-American community, among others, were buried there. Linden Grove Cemetery now boasts more than 22,000 burials on twenty-two acres. Although it has traditionally been an African-American graveyard, it has been integrated for many years. It is the oldest and most historically significant cemetery in Covington.

Interred in Linden Grove are a number of well-known historical figures, including William Wright Southgate (US Representative), who was laid to rest in 1849. Dr. Adam D. Kelly, one of Covington's first physicians, is also interred here.

Among its more well-known burials is that of Charles Bennett. Mr. Bennett was buried here in 1938, followed by his wife one year later. He was a security guard for more than thirty years in life, and local legend says that he is still a guard to this day. He is known around the Westside neighborhood as "the Guard of Linden Grove" as his ghostly presence has often been seen standing guard at the gateway into the historic graveyard. Those who see him describe him as a formidable figure of impeccable style. Mr. Bennett has been reported to be wearing a dark blue uniform with thin gold bands around the cuffs, a bright red tie, and black leather shoes polished to a high mirror shine. Winter or summer, hot or frigid, no nefarious spirit dares to desecrate the burials in Linden Grove, dare they meet the fiercely unwavering bravery of Mr. Bennett, "the Guard of Linden Grove."

CHAPTER EIGHT

Oak Hill Cemetery

The Weird Guy

A strange tale of supernatural proportions
unfolded here in Oak Hill Cemetery.

In the middle years of the twentieth century Glendale was a great place to raise a family. The small town of Glendale, a northern suburb of Cincinnati, boasted spacious lawns and nice neighborhoods. The streets were safe and the schools were good. Folks knew each other and a friend was never far away. The folks gathered at the park near the soda fountain after church. It was the kind of place that those prone to nostalgia remember fondly.

As with most of the Midwest in the early 1950s, the economy was booming, and the possibilities seemed endless. Glendale was, in those years, a perfect blend of country and city life. One could find plenty of open spaces, while still enjoying the amenities of a bigger city. Manufacturing and entry-level management jobs were easy to find. The warm summers meant playing in the yard, while winter snow meant sledding over the hills. Glendale seemed perfect, with one strange exception: the weird guy.

No one seemed to know his name, much less anything conclusive about him, only that he had hung around Glendale for as long as anyone could remember. He was always alone. Most people ignored him, but every once in a while someone would try to engage him. He never responded in a normal manner, and most people thought that he was strange, or perhaps mentally deficient. He dressed in well-worn, but not shabby, clothes. People would occasionally give him money or a leftover sandwich from the local diner, but most of the time he just stood on the street corners staring blankly off into the distance. By all accounts, he was impervious to the weather, standing around sometimes in near-blizzard conditions. The weird guy would, from time to time, be seen lurking around the alleys late at night. He never bothered anyone directly, and the cops left him alone, writing him off as a homeless man but not a criminal threat. The neighbors, though, gossiped about him on a regular basis.

Eventually, the weird guy's presence in Glendale wove itself into the fabric of the community. He was, to most residents . . . invisible.

Things in Glendale were quiet until the morning of March 11, 1951. On that chilly morning, not far from the local movie theatre, a little girl was found murdered. Her name was Lucy Pickins, and she was just ten years old. She'd had her head nearly cut off with what appeared to be a large kitchen knife. The coroner also located several other cuts and abrasions on her body. At the time of her death, she wore a light blue dress with a white ruffled collar that was soaked in blood. A toy she was known to carry was also found near the body.

Her parents, when informed, were inconsolable, and the police chief promised them a full investigation. The story of little Lucy's murder made headlines in the evening edition of the local papers. The Pickinses were flooded with calls and visits from concerned neighbors. A church vigil was held the next afternoon, and Lucy was the talk of the town.

When the clock struck noon on March 13, a large crowd gathered to hear an update from the local police chief. In a ten-minute address, he laid out the known facts in the case.

He glanced down at his notes as he angrily admitted that the killer was still at large. The reaction from the crowd was swift and visceral. They wanted action, and they wanted it now! The chief tried his best to calm everyone down, but by then the crowd was beginning to turn into a mob. At the edge of the gathering, a visibly agitated man paced back and forth before his rhythm was broken by another man pushing through the crowd. The man came forward from the direction of the movie theatre screaming: "The weird guy, the weird guy did it!" Soon, everyone was wildly chanting: "The weird guy did it!"

The police chief ordered calm.

But by then, it was too late. The crowd had heard the accusation and its collective mind was off and running. Like the pulsing of an octopus, the mob moved and stirred as one. Emotions were running high. Fathers joined mothers, and the old joined the young. Chants of "Get the weird guy!" could be heard echoing up and down the streets. The mob spread out, more people joined in, and they began to head to the block where the weird guy most often hung out. When the mob came around the corner, there he was. The weird guy was standing on his usual corner, staring off into space and minding his own business. In just a matter of seconds, the mob had encircled the weird guy and enveloped him. The crowd swelled and lurched. Looking over the crowd, one could see sticks and fists raised up in the air. Shouts and screams of torment could be heard from both the crowd and the weird guy. In a few minutes' time, the mob was broken up by a large police squad. The mob scattered and stirred around. Everyone was yelling and it seemed for that moment like a normally quiet Glendale had erupted into madness.

When the mob finally dispersed at the urging of the cops, the weird guy lay nearly dead on the sidewalk. Blood was gushing out of a large gash on the side of his head onto the perfectly manicured green grass. His left hand was crushed and twitching like a nervous sinner before the priest. Air bubbled up out of his lungs through the open wound on his torso. Officer Blatt yelped as he felt the weird guy's blood creeping into his right shoe. At length, an ambulance was called, but the weird guy was dead before it arrived. He died right there on the sidewalk in front of everyone.

The Glendale police department opened an inquiry into the day's events. A man was dead, and the chief wanted answers. For now, whether he was guilty or not was beside the point; he had unlawfully been killed by the mob and someone was guilty of that. They wanted to know who had been directly responsible for the weird guy's death.

The local coroner took the body down to the morgue for an autopsy. For the next several hours the police questioned everyone who had been in the mob. But suspects were few. Most of the cops could only remember one or two people they'd recognized in the rogue crowd. Those ten or eleven people were brought in for questioning; each claiming that they were only a spectator to the actual killing. Physical evidence was nearly useless. Blood was smeared, footprints were indistinguishable, and no fingerprints could be lifted from the rocks and sticks found at the scene. It was going to be old-fashioned police work, or dumb luck, that would crack this case.

The killing of the weird guy made all the papers the next morning, and the chief was as determined as ever to close the books on this one. The officers kept questioning people and going over their recollections of the day.

One officer soon realized that there was no proof to the allegation, and that the crowd had gotten out of control due to the reckless accusation. The chief ordered his men to question the accuser to try and ascertain where he'd gotten the notion. The accuser was identified and escorted by several policemen down to the station. The officers and the accuser got to talking and the conversation ran late into the night. Several cops came in to speak with him as they slowly began to put a picture together of what happened. One of the cops remembered that while passing by the theatre windows he saw a movie poster in the window for a new movie: *The Man from Planet X*. He also noticed the subtitle, "The weirdest visitor the earth has ever seen!"

The cop pulled the man up by the lapels, putting his face in the accuser's face, and said, "Hey, I noticed you came up by the theatre today. I noticed you were looking at the poster in the window just before you made the accusation against the weird guy. Was that because you had just read the words "weirdest visitor" on the movie poster? Are you getting our case mixed up with a movie in your mind? Do you think the weird guy is some kind of alien killer from outer space? . . . Well, do you?" The accuser just smirked at the officer, and he was let go.

The case of the weird guy just seemed to be a dead end. The autopsy revealed nothing that wasn't obvious at the scene. No conclusive evidence could be produced, and no arrest was made. The chief was not happy. He had two unsolved deaths on his books, and that did not suit him.

The chief didn't know whether the accuser had been right, but he also believed in the motto: Innocent until proven guilty. So for now, the weird guy was innocent in the eyes of the law. The chief asked the state to bury the weird guy and give him some sort of proper funeral and burial in Oak Hill Cemetery.

He was buried with a generic funeral. The casket was lowered into an unmarked grave, for they knew not the man's name or religious tradition. They did not know where he was from or when he was born. They only knew a death date. A small wooden cross was erected as a church bell off in the distance sounded its deathly knell. Oak Hill took on an eerie silence.

The incident with the weird guy left a palpable moroseness in the air around northern Cincinnati. Neighbors were afraid to talk for fear their conversations might be interpreted as guilt. The police, meanwhile, were working overtime trying to solve the double murders, but the chief had clearly put the emphasis back on the murder of little Lucy. The two murders had left a split among the people, with half of them thinking that a child killer still roamed free, while the other half felt that, most likely, the weird guy was guilty after all, had paid the price, and that the case of Lucy's killing was solved. Still, the public was clamoring for results as fears of a child killer began to rise among the populace again.

Just over one week later, the "Who did it?" debate was settled. The body of another little girl was found not far from the Oak Hill Cemetery gates. The little girl, Abigail Booker, had been murdered in exactly the same manner as Lucy Pickins. A clean slice had nearly taken off her head. The news sent the public into hysterics. The streets of Glendale became a ghost town. The police chief was at the end of his rope, but not the killer. Then, at long last, someone dared to ask the obvious questions: "Was the weird guy innocent?" and "Were the two child killings linked?"

The police had no answers.

The police continued to investigate. The mayor was breathing down the chief's neck, and the public wanted an arrest. Witness after witness was brought in for questioning. Several people reported a suspicious character hanging around the night of Abigail's murder; however, no accurate description could be made of the stranger. Every tip was combed through. The few leads they had were assiduously followed to their ends. Some very strange witness accounts were recorded, but none stranger than the ones that stated they had seen a ghostly figure floating near where Abigail Booker's body had been found. The ghostly figure of . . . the weird guy. At first the police just laughed off the sightings of the weird guy's ghost as just hysteria, but as more witnesses came forward, they all confirmed the sighting. Was it more than mere coincidence?

A ghost story was an amusing antidote for a newspaper column or local gossip, but it did not solve a murder. After a month on the books, the police were no closer to catching either killer than they had ever been. The pressure was rising, and confidence was falling. A few days passed, but still the little girl's murders remained a mystery.

At the end of April, another young girl's body was found near the railroad tracks. Her name was Florence Turning. She was found murdered in the same manner as the other two girls, with her head nearly decapitated. She also showed signs of injuries elsewhere on her body. Mrs. Turning, upon hearing the news of her daughter's murder, went into hysterics. She completely broke down. Mr. Turning tried to keep a stiff upper lip, but one could tell he was in a deep state of shock. The police chief promised the Turnings that they would do everything they could to bring the killer to justice.

The next morning, the police held a press conference to update local media of the latest developments. One reporter asked the question everyone had on their minds, but no one had been willing to ask. Did Cincinnati have a serial child killer in their midst? The reporters also asked questions about the ghost of the weird guy and about the suspicious character that had been seen hanging around Abigail's murder. The police reported that they had also seen a "person of interest" skulking around, but most of the men just wrote him off as an onlooker. As for the ghost, "Well . . .," said the cop conducting the press conference, "some of us think there might be something to it, but most of us think it's a reaction of mania by an uneasy public; but no one's laughing at the witnesses." He went on to state how everyone was on edge and that the whole town wanted the killer to be caught. No arrests had been made, and the evidence was still being sifted through. The press conference went on for more than an hour, but the answers seemed more like platitudes than statements of genuine progress.

Apparently, the specter of the weird guy was the talk of the town. While some folks discussed the evidence, most were nervously chatting about the ghost of the weird guy. Everyone was on edge about a subject that was frightening and unpleasant, and to most a ghost story was an easy way to communicate.

People kept their children inside and their doors locked tight. Church trips and the spring dance at the elementary school were cancelled. Even though the warmer days of spring had come, Glendale was living indoors in fear. Most men in the neighborhood spent their evenings peeking out through the curtains and checking doors to make sure they were locked. Meanwhile, most women held their young ones close and read them happy children's books full of princesses and horses. Parents exchanged nervous glances while they tried their best not to upset the children of Glendale. The police continued to receive calls about strangers on the streets every few minutes.

A graveside funeral was held for Florence Turning at Oak Hill Cemetery, and nearly the whole town showed up to pay their respects and show support for the Turning family. A special task force had been assigned the duty of watching people at the funeral for any suspicious activity. None was reported.

The investigation ground onward. The entire police department was at its wits' end. No substantial evidence was pointing to anyone. In fact, the only consistent reports were that of the ghost of the weird guy floating around the scene where Abigail's body had been found. An exhausted panic waved through the citizens of Glendale. People were beginning to wonder if anyone would ever be caught. Neighborhood associations had begun to form "night watch" patrols to help the police keep extra eyes out. The problem was that as the investigation dragged on, neighbors began to suspect neighbors. The town of Glendale felt like it was frozen in place. The public's resolve was strong, and the policemen were willing to work the overtime; something had to be done.

Not long after young Florence Turning had been laid to rest, a break in the cases came. But, it came in the oddest of manners. Someone accused the ghost of the weird guy of murder!

The whole idea seemed absurd. A ghost can't kill anyone; or can it? While a number of policemen dismissed the idea outright, several of the men thought there might just be something to it. The chief, at the end of his own ideas, decided that though he thought it was silly, he would allow a discussion about the possibility of a killer ghost. The first question raised was: If the weird guy had still been alive when Lucy was murdered, it could not have been his ghost that did it. The ghost question did not answer for Lucy, unless the murders were unrelated. The majority of the cops, including the chief, believed that all three were related. The "all related" theory let the weird guy off the hook for all of the murders. If the weird guy was just lying peacefully in his grave, the police could get on with their work. It was obvious that the ghost of the weird guy knew something; but what? There was only one way to find out the answer to that question. The Glendale Police Department needed to hold a séance!

A search was conducted for someone to lead the séance, a person qualified to raise the spirits of the dead. This was going to involve more than just a quick spin on the Spirit Board; no parlor game was going to help them solve a string of murders. A couple of days and a few false starts later, the perfect person, László Zövér, was brought in to conduct the séance. Zövér, a native of the Carpathian Mountains, was well known among spiritualists and parapsychologists in Cincinnati. If anyone could legitimately raise the spirit of the weird guy, it was László Zövér.

Some parameters were set up, and a small group was selected to attend the séance. It was to be held at the weird guy's grave, at midnight. The mayors of both Glendale and Cincinnati, two of the area's top detectives, as well as the police chief were in attendance. A large crowd had gathered just outside of the cemetery gates in anticipation of the night's events. The crowd included the parents of the three murdered girls, as well as many of those who gave statements to the police. With the men gathered and the moon shining brightly . . . the séance commenced.

Zövér started by asking for absolute silence from everyone, before rolling his eyes backwards and transitioning to an oddly relaxed state. He began to chant in a low baritone, with the chanting getting steadily louder. Zövér extended his arms out over the grave, fingers arched as if they were circling a crystal ball. Off in the distance, a young boy began to beat a steady rhythm on a drum. The mood at the grave became more and more intense. In a low voice that mimicked the tone of the chant, Zövér began to speak to the weird guy, assuring him that he was a friend and that he meant him no harm. As the attendees stood in amazement, Zövér kept on talking with the deceased. He asked the weird guy a question and waited patiently for an answer. In a few moments, he nodded his head and proceeded to ask another question.

The question and answer period went on for some time. Several long minutes in, one of the detectives leaned over to the chief and asked in a whisper, "Why all the Q and A?" The chief whispered back, "He needs to establish trust with the deceased."

Zövér transitioned back into the chanting, while continuing to move his hands over the grave. All of a sudden the night air became thick and began to swirl as if a violent storm was imminent. The men had to hold their hats and plant their feet more firmly on the ground. The atmosphere around the men began to move in waves as if they were looking through the heat rising off a stove. A pack of dogs began to howl somewhere near the cemetery fence. Birds that had been perched in the nearby trees flew off. The moon was full and bright, and those in attendance could make out every blade of new grass twitching on the weird guy's grave. The ground around their feet began to move . . .

All of a sudden, a pure white fog slithered out of the earth and low across the cemetery grounds. It curled itself around the ankles of the men. The light of the moon danced in and out and around and through the fog. . . .And then the fog began to slowly rise, taking form as it ascended upward. Soon the foggy diaphanous form of a man glided around them. The men, normally fearless, recoiled in terror at the sight before them. Zövér waved his hands out at the ghostly figure and commanded its attention. He then began to speak with the specter. At first, he introduced himself and then proceeded to ask the weird guy's ghost some questions.

The first question from Zövér was: "Oh spirit, I beseech you tell me who it was that murdered you? Who was it that delivered the fatal blow upon your head?" The men who were gathered around stared in awe at the ghostly figure. The swirling white fog stretched out as if its arm was unfolding. A hand-shaped configuration of fog spilled out from the ghost's ever-extending reach. The fingers at the end of the hand had an eerie skeletal quality to them as they pointed a finger towards the cemetery gate. Zövér replied to the ghost, "The gate? Is it someone standing at the gate?" The foggy spectral figure looked down upon Zövér and said clearly, "Igen." Zövér stared at the ghost in amazement, not expecting it to answer him in his native Hungarian. He looked at the men gathered around him and said, "The ghost of the weird guy answered me, but in my native Hungarian. He confirmed that his killer is, in fact, standing at the gates to the cemetery." The men all looked at the gate.

The chief told Zövér, "Ask it about the girls." No sooner had Zövér asked the ghost who had been responsible for killing the three little girls, than the ghostly fog began to move towards the cemetery gates. "What shall we do?" asked one of the men. The Mayor of Glendale answered, "Follow it, of course."

The men followed the eerie fog across the cemetery grounds towards the large gate. While the men sidestepped headstones, the translucent fog passed through them.

The enormous gates were locked, but the fog moved through them with ease and swirled around through the large crowd gathered there. It took the cemetery manager a few minutes to get the heavy lock opened, and the gate swung back in order to let the men out.

Once the men were out and standing in front of the gate, the crowd dispersed and fell back, giving the ghostly fog plenty of room to move throughout the people standing there. By the time enough lanterns had been lit to adequately see what was happening, the police and the detectives saw that the foggy apparition was hanging heavily over one man who was crouched downward. The ghost's skeletal hands reached down and grabbed the man by his shoulders and lifted him into the air. A look of sheer terror passed across the man's face just before he passed out and went limp. The men who had attended the séance had nearly the same look of terror on their own faces as they watched the ghost turn towards Zövér.

He simply stared at the ghost. The fog heaved, "This is the man who killed the three little girls: Lucy, Abigail, and Florence! For I witnessed it myself. He was also the one who struck the final blow that sent me to this ghostly realm." Zövér and the police listened carefully, and a quick-thinking officer jotted down the words uttered by the ghostly fog.

The ghost of the weird guy continued, "He murdered the first little girl, Lucy, after trying unsuccessfully to give her candy and take her away. He grabbed the second little girl, Abigail, in a store while her mother looked the other way. He killed her when she began to scream. He came in through an unlocked window in little Florence's room and took her from her bed. He killed her for fear of being caught. . . . and as for me, he killed me in the chaos of the mob that he intentionally created because I had witnessed his first murder. He needed to get rid of me before I told anyone."

At this point, Zövér interrupted the ghost, "Intentionally created? What do you mean by that?"

The ghost of the weird guy replied to Zövér, "I mean he shouted the accusation to divert you all from himself to me, knowing that a mob will do and believe nearly anything it's told to do! He preyed on people's fear and outrage at the murder."

The chief then stepped forward, grabbed the man on the pavement and lifted him up, exposing his face to the light of the lanterns. He screamed as he realized that it was the same man who had first made the accusation against the weird guy at the movie theatre. The man who had cried, "The weird guy did it!"

When the chief looked up, the ghostly fog had vanished into the darkness of the night. László Zövér, too, had vanished into thin air.

The police chief had a suspect and an accusation. But, he had learned the hard way that an accusation was not evidence. So, he decided to arrest the man on charges of suspicion of murder and disorderly conduct; that way he could hold him for a few days while he conducted a proper inquiry. He put handcuffs on the man and led him to his patrol car. The chief ordered his men to investigate, and he also got personally involved in the case.

The suspect was safe and sound behind bars, and the chief, wanting no more trouble, convened a thorough and by-the-book investigation. They utilized all the latest techniques, and a couple of months later the man, whose name turned out to be Jurek Stadtmann, was put on trial for four counts of first-degree murder.

The trial was as grueling as it was fantastic. Jury members were hard to find, as everyone anywhere near Glendale had read about the case in the newspaper. A jury was eventually seated, and Jurek Stadtmann was given a public defender. The trial started, and opening statements were offered by both the prosecution and the defense. Each day at trial the courtroom's galley was packed to capacity. The public and the press alike filled the hallways outside the courtroom. The prosecutor presented evidence from the police investigation, and the public defender did his best to refute it. Harsh words and damning evidence were exchanged for several days. The public defender asked why anyone would take as evidence the word of a ghost. The prosecutor countered with the fact that the police had followed up on everything the ghost of the weird guy had said. They were not resting on the word of a ghost, but rather on hard facts obtained through rigorous police work. Times and dates were combed over assiduously. Physical evidence was presented. Wood chips and blood were compared, as well as several photographs.

The character of the police chief was questioned, but the judge dismissed the attempted character assassination quickly. The prosecutor made hay out of the fact that the public defender was young and this was his first "real" murder trial. It was obvious the two men did not like each other very much.

The press had a field day with both the prosecutor and the accused. While most residents took the trial very seriously, some strange side questions and stories regarding the case began to circulate. What had become of László Zövér? Why was he not around for the trial? One funny story that emerged said that the alien from the movie poster had, through telepathy, taken over Jurek Stadtmann's brain and that was what had made him go mad.

During the prosecutor's closing statements, he asked the members of the jury a question: "What does it say about Mr. Stadtmann's guilt that there have been no more murders during the time he's been in custody?" The public defender had no argument to counter that question. At the conclusion of day eight, both sides rested, and the onus was placed on the jury to deliberate.

The jury took only two days to return a verdict.

GUILTY!

Cheers erupted among the crowds both inside and outside the courtroom. The headlines were in bold type, and a collective sigh of relief waved over the town of Glendale. Newspaper commentary and local gossip went on for several days as the public parsed the case for themselves.

A few days later, the formal sentencing was held. The occasion was somber. All were told to rise, and everyone held their breath in anticipation. The judge read the sentence aloud: "Jurek Stadtmann, it is the judgment of this court that you are to die for the crimes of which you are convicted. You are to be taken from this place and hung by your neck until you are dead. May God have mercy on your soul."

Cheers again broke out! The headline of the afternoon edition simply read: "DEATH for Stadtmann"!

Appeals from the public defender quickly failed, and on a bitterly cold day in January 1952, Jurek Stadtmann was unceremoniously hanged for the murders of Lucy Pickins, Abigail Booker, Florence Turning, and the weird guy.

No family or friends had visited Stadtmann while he was in jail or on trial. No one claimed his body after the execution. He was buried in an unmarked grave in an undisclosed location.

The ghost of the weird guy was never seen or heard from again.

CHAPTER NINE

Spring Grove Cemetery

John R. Hugh

Local legend says that any visitor to the grave of John R. Hugh can raise his spirit through performing a supernatural ritual.

John R. Hugh was born in northern Wales on July 28, 1855. Famine was scarring the Welsh countryside in the mid-1800s, and his father, Robert Hugh, wanted to find a more prosperous country in which to raise his family. They set out for America when John was just four years old. Upon arriving in America, Robert Hugh purchased a large parcel of land in Kentucky. He was going to raise tobacco with the help of slaves. The commencement of the Civil War, though, interrupted his plans. His tobacco farm was never planted and he could not provide for his family. Confederate soldiers moving through the area stole or confiscated everything in his gardens and storerooms. The two slaves he had purchased vanished in the confusion, never to be seen again. He lost everything. His wife found him in an old abandoned barn, dead from a self-inflicted gunshot wound to the head. Annabelle Hugh was a widow at the age of twenty-nine. John was a fatherless child at eight years old.

Annabelle had no choice but to remarry again quickly, for she needed the support. But by 1865, the country was in shambles. The president was dead, and men were scarce. It seemed that old men and young boys were all that was left after the war ended. Annabelle and John were left to beg on the streets, take odd jobs, and do anything they could to survive. Her English had a strong Welsh accent to it, making her hard to understand, leading a lot of people to think she was slow. Regular employment seemed a dream.

At the age of fifteen John found his mother dead. She had been violated and murdered outside of the flophouse where they resided. He was on his own.

For a time, he indulged in petty thievery and conning to get by, but in time he began to think of a tradesman's job. He headed north to the Ohio River, hoping to get work on a boat or at the wharf. He found out quickly that he did not like the river life, and headed into the burgeoning city of Cincinnati. There he found work as an assistant butler in a large home owned by the Sieseby family. He liked the job and they liked him. The head butler was a man named Donald, and the two of them got along. Things went on like this for about four years before Donald became very ill one winter's day. Everyone thought that it was just a cold, but it turned quickly to pneumonia. Donald died on a Tuesday in February. John was immediately promoted to head butler and was allowed to hire one assistant.

Late one evening, after everyone else had supposedly gone to bed, John overheard some people in the living room. He thought at first they might be burglars, so he crept slowly to the pocket doors and peeked carefully through. What he saw at first startled him and then made him curious. Sitting around a large table that normally was not there sat the Siesebys and two other couples he did not recognize. They were dressed in black and sat deathly still, bathed in the flickering candlelight. It was not John's practice to eavesdrop or spy, but his curiosity took over and he found himself watching against his better judgment. Soon, Mrs. Sieseby raised her hands and began to chant an odd chant that John had heard somewhere before. It reminded him of his mother. As the chant continued, he realized that he was watching a séance. They were trying to contact the spirit of someone who had died. Just then, John felt a cold breeze wrap its way around his neck; he spun around only to see his mother's ghostly presence before him. He let out a scream that would have woken any spirits not already awakened by the séance. John woke in his own bed the next morning. The prior night's events were never spoken of out loud. Over the next few years, a number of other strange things occurred in the house.

A few years later, Mrs. Sieseby walked into the dining room to find John circling the table while rubbing his hands vigorously together. She asked him what he was doing, and he replied that he was performing a supernatural ritual to calm himself. When she asked him to explain, she received a rather tepid response.

"Well, Ma'am, I've had a hard life. My mama and my pa both died when I was young, and I ain't never had no good luck, 'cept getting hired here. Well, sometimes I just get sad, and so I rub my hands and walk in circles to calm myself. My mama taught me how to do it. I do it to cheer myself up." He then looked up at Mrs. Sieseby. "Do you think that's weird, Ma'am?" he asked. "No, I think that's a fine thing to do to raise your spirits," she replied. "I believe in raising one's spirits. You go right ahead."

In the late winter of 1883–1884, John R. Hugh got sick. He languished in bed for several days before dying of a fever on March 28, 1884. John had been on staff for the Sieseby family for more than a decade when he passed. It was his whole life. He never married or had any children. Mr. and Mrs. Sieseby paid for him to be buried in the side section of Spring Grove Cemetery. They even paid for him to have a funeral and a marker for his grave.

Local legend says that the story does not end there.

It turned out that because the Siesebys practiced black magic and necromancy, and were into all sorts of dark rituals and séances, they believed that John was still with them in spirit form. According to haunted local lore, in the years after that, Mr. and Mrs. Sieseby would go to John's grave. There, they would walk circles around it while vigorously rubbing their hands. A passerby once asked them what they were doing, and Mrs. Sieseby replied, "Raising a spirit."

Even today, locals say, if you walk circles around the grave of John R. Hugh while rubbing your hands fast and steady, that you too may raise his spirit.

CHAPTER TEN

Spring Grove Cemetery

The Gate: That Which Enters Never Leaves

The funeral carriage entrance gate at Spring Grove Cemetery. Several ghostly spirits are said to be entangled in this gate.

As one stands facing the immense gates that lead into the Spring Grove Cemetery, one cannot help but be in awe. It is massive—majestic, beautiful, and haunting. The gate stands in guard against anyone or anything that may want to surreptitiously enter the grounds. They also keep that which has entered from leaving. As they say: .the departed remain.

The gates are more than just a device to control the coming and goings of the living, though. They are a passageway for the dead—a one-way passage. For all those departed this earthly life and brought within these gates, they are forever home: a gated community for the dead, so to speak.

Lugubrious-looking on a dismal winter's day, the Norman Chapel that sits just beyond the gates is a receiving place for those brought in the funeral carriages of days long gone. As the funeral procession arrives, the gates swing open and the horse-drawn carriage carrying the casket slowly moves along the ruts in the road. When it has pulled through the gates, they are shut on the deceased for the last time. The funeral carriage draws up beneath the canopy at the chapel doors. The casket is unloaded into the chapel so the grieving families may have their time of mourning. At the conclusion of the funeral, the casket is reloaded into the creaky horse-drawn wagon and taken down what is historically known as "Casket Road" to its final resting place. A casket is very much a type of gate, a point of final closure. . . .And so it has been at Spring Grove Cemetery ever since the first interment took place there on September 1, 1845.

The funeral carriage is then allowed to leave the cemetery grounds back through the intimidating gates and is permitted to return to its funeral home. The corpse it left behind, though—never again to pass through the gates. There is disagreement as to what happens to the ghost of the deceased. Some say the ghost remains with the body in the grave and that this is why cemeteries are haunted. Others say that once the body is laid deep within the grave, that the ghost, or soul if you prefer, is free to wander about the world, unencumbered by the heft of a locked iron gate. One may argue that this is all just geography and that the only thing between here and there are the gates of apprehension, or one may simply accept that they have entered a realm *beyond* conventional geography.

One need only ask the victims of the influenza outbreak that gripped the city of Cincinnati from 1918–1919. The epidemic started in Boston in August, but quickly spread to the Midwest. Panic descended right alongside the disease, and before it was over, near the end of 1919, city health officials estimated that over 1,500 people had succumbed to influenza. Oddly enough, the city's wealthiest areas were hit the hardest; many former residents were brought through the enormous gate at Spring Grove Cemetery. Some of them, the survivors say, are still wandering around, looking for a cure.

The main gate, just down from the Norman Chapel gate, is an imposing one as well—a passageway for those who bring flowers to their departed loved ones. It, too, is a curtain into a realm far more certain than our own. When one enters through the main gates to Spring Grove Cemetery, they could not be faulted for being impressed with the Gothic Victorian architecture that lends its ambiance so well to the fears of the mortal. Equal parts church edifice and English horror movie set, the majesty of Spring Grove's gates and buildings prepare one to enter the world of the immortal.

CHAPTER ELEVEN

Spring Grove Cemetery

Paranormal Investigation

Alice's grave in Spring Grove Cemetery—this photograph is believed to have been taken during a paranormal investigation.

On a Saturday night in early January 2013, Jenny Albarini decided to invite some friends over to watch a movie. She invited her two best friends, Minnie Schiffani and Rosa Alvarez, who brought along their two boyfriends, Ron Benson and Juan Martin. They were also joined by a friend of Juan's, Mick Yelkin, whom they all knew from school. The group arrived promptly at 6:00 p.m., and they immediately began to chat and dig into the chips and salsa that Jenny had laid out. They joked about school, got caught up on what all their friends were doing, and shared the latest things they had seen on social media. Juan and Ron, who were teammates on the local baseball team, began to trade friendly jabs about who had more home runs the prior season. The three girls talked about clothes and their grades, while Mick just stared at Jenny while working up some excuse to ask her out. The group bantered about the neighborhood and what colleges they were thinking about attending. Jenny turned on the stereo, and they listened to CDs for a while. Mrs. Albarini, Jenny's mother, brought in more chips, salsa, soft drinks, and some sandwiches.

By the time they got around to deciding on a movie, it was well after 7:30 p.m. Jenny had a huge collection of movies, and each friend gave his or her opinion on them. Mick and Ron wanted to watch a sci-fi film, while Rosa and Minnie wanted to watch an action drama. Jenny said she didn't care, and neither did Juan. The group could not come to a consensus on what movie to watch, and so, they decided instead to just sit around and enjoy each other's company and the robust conversation.

In just a short time, the group had talked about everything from parents to the political situation in the Middle East. While there was plenty of silliness and flirting in the conversation, they also took each subject seriously. Mick shared that he had recently had his heart broken by Belle McAllen. He expected the group to laugh at him, but surprisingly enough, they didn't snicker. Jenny replied, "Yeah, I've had my heart broken, too." Ron remarked that this was better than any movie. The group agreed, and then they each began to share their favorite movie or TV show. They all agreed they liked the paranormal investigation shows, even if some of them were kind of cheesy. Mick glanced over at Jenny, just to see how she folded her legs on the couch.

The group talked at length about their favorite paranormal TV show, with each of them chiming in about what they liked or disliked about the programs. They shared how the stories on TV made them feel, with Rosa seeming to be the most timid and Mick the most bold. Jenny claimed to have some level of paranormal sensibilities, and Minnie and Ron agreed. Juan said he had sensed something in his house and conducted his own paranormal investigation. He said he found that a spirit was haunting his house, but that it was friendly and quiet most of the time, and so he had decided against an exorcism.

When the clock chimed 10:00 p.m., Jenny's mother popped in to see how things were going and to tell them she was going to bed. Minnie asked

Mrs. Albarini if she had ever experienced anything paranormal, or weird in a supernatural way. Mrs. Albarini's face grew solemn. The six high school friends grew quiet and curious. She replied that yes, she knew a ghost story, because this one had happened to her. Rosa pulled up a chair, and Ron turned the lights down. Mrs. Albarini sat slowly, letting an ominous mood settle over the room. The six friends were enraptured.

"Well," Mrs. Albarini said, her tone of voice changing from its usual fast pace to a slow deliberate cadence, "Where do I begin?"

She went on to recall a strange story from her youth twenty-three years prior.

She and two friends had been out driving around the Ohio countryside when it began to get dark. There was a fine mist of rain coming down, and the girls knew they needed to head back to town. They turned onto O'Bannonville Road heading west. Just as they started onto the Little Miami River Bridge in Loveland, they saw a young girl standing in the rain near the railing. It looked as if she were going to jump into the river. Sianne, the girl driving the car, hit the brakes and slid to a stop just in front of the girl on the bridge. The three girls got out of their car and started to approach the girl. She was wearing a long white nightgown, and her pale yellow locks of hair fell down like a noose around her neck. She had a stoic look of nothingness upon her face. Her skin was as white as her nightgown. The girl seemed to shine in an unearthly manner. The three girls spoke to her, but she did not respond; she just stared at them in the oddest of ways. "I begged her not to jump, and asked her if she was lost," added Mrs. Albarini. The girls just stared at her and then at each other; they had never seen anything like this before. At length, they decided that the girl must be "out of it" in some way—drunk, sick, or mentally disabled. The three girls asked each other what they should do. They decided to grab the girl and take her to their house where they could find out who she was and contact her family. The three girls approached the other girl and grabbed her. But, as soon as they touched her, she vanished into the misty night air. The three girls stood on the bridge alone.

Over the next couple of weeks the three girls told several people about the girl on the bridge. Some of them laughed it off as a funny story, but some took them seriously. One of the women who heard the story told them to come with her. She took them to an old man named Mr. Graun who hung around the local library. There, at the behest of the woman, the girls related the story to Mr. Graun. He listened carefully, digesting every word. When they were finished, the man clarified a few points as he leaned in and told them that it was not their imagination; there *was* such a girl. He said that his father, while a boy, had known that girl, and told him stories about those days. Her name was Alice, and she had died in the late 1800s while playing near that bridge. Alice had fallen off the railing and drowned before anyone could get her out of the water. Mr.

Graun said that his father had witnessed the incident and had never forgotten it. His father's story had haunted him for years.

Alice's family had been beside themselves with grief, as she was their only daughter. The family laid young Alice to rest in the Spring Grove Cemetery, placing a scroll-style headstone to commemorate her life. The old man's father had taken him there several times to visit with what the father called "his childhood friend, Alice." He said that even after all these years the story of Alice still haunted him.

The old man told the three girls that the ghost of Alice wandered along the railing of the bridge looking for the life she had lost so many years before. The ghost they had seen that night was the ghost of the little girl, Alice.

At that moment, Mrs. Albarini rolled her head around slowly. She opened her eyes and smiled a sardonic grin at the group of friends gathered in the living room.

They were all just staring at her in amazement.

"I never knew that story, Mom," said Jenny.

"Wow, Mrs. Albarini, that's some story," chimed in Ron.

Rosa and Minnie just stared at the others with a look of shock on their faces.

Juan said, "I've driven over that bridge, I know where it is. I always thought it had something weird about it, but I never knew the back story."

...And almost as quickly as she had entered the room, Mrs. Albarini was gone.

The six friends could talk of nothing else except the story they had just been told. Juan was the first to say that they should investigate it. "I've got a good handheld videocam," he said.

Ron said, "My dad's got some high-end audio recorders I think he'll let us use."

The six friends decided they were going to become a paranormal investigation team. "Maybe we can do this, and I can write a term paper on the results," stated Minnie.

Everyone agreed that she was the best writer in the group, and that a paper would be a great way of wrapping up the investigation.

Rosa said, "Maybe we'll even get on TV and become famous!"

Everyone laughed.

Jenny asked Mick to come sit next to her, and the group of friends began to lay out their paranormal investigation plan.

They had to include the bridge and the gravesite at Spring Grove Cemetery. Ron volunteered to interview the son of the old man. Jenny said she'd see if she could get any more information out of her mom. They thought it best to wait until the next weekend to do the filming, so that they could stay out late.

In the meantime, Ron went to interview the son of the old man. He wanted to hear the story for himself, and see if he could get any more details. Juan tagged along to film. At Mr. Graun's house, the two friends found the old man's son sitting in the corner of the main room reading the paper. They approached him politely and asked him if they could speak with him about Alice. He was more than amicable. Juan set up the camera, and Ron put a microphone on the son's lapel. When they were ready, the old man's son told the story just as Jenny's mom had relayed it. Ron asked him a few questions about the case, but just like a copy of a copy, the details had gotten a bit fuzzy over the years. He did, however, note that he thought it strange that Alice was buried alone with no other family members with her. He pondered why it might be that neither her parents, or any siblings, were buried with her. Ron and Juan thanked the man for his help and left.

They both remarked that it had been, by and large, a useless endeavor. "We do, though, need to follow up on why she was buried alone," remarked Juan.

"Yes, that is curious," said Ron.

A few nights later the group met at Jenny's house to go over their checklist and finalize plans. When everything was ready they headed out to the bridge over the Little Miami River in the small community of Loveland. Temperatures were already below freezing, and a light snow was falling. It was just after 6:30 p.m., and the sky was dark, but the light off the snow made it almost as light as daytime. They parked at the brick building on the nearest corner, deciding it was best to walk the block up onto the bridge. Juan started recording just as they got to the foot of the bridge.

Minnie was designated as "the interviewer." She was a pretty and articulate young woman, and everyone thought she would look best on camera. Minnie began the first filmed segment with a short introduction to the story they were investigating. Rosa held an umbrella over the camera while Ron fiddled with some audio equipment. Soon Minnie pulled Jenny into the frame and asked her about her mother's experience with Alice. Jenny and Minnie spoke for over nine minutes before everyone decided that it was getting cold. Rosa suggested they go back to the car to warm up. Juan agreed, but wanted to film one quick segment over the bridge first. He walked over the bridge, followed closely by Rosa, and back while filming. Ron stayed close to record anything out of the ordinary. Meanwhile, Mick, Jenny, and Minnie looked around. A few minutes later, the group went back to the car. Once in the car, Mick and Jenny curled up next to each other. Ron smirked at them, and Jenny said, "We just want to get warm."

"Hot is more like it," quipped Ron, smiling. The friends all laughed.

In the car, the group shared their experiences on the bridge, and looked anxiously into the small video screen at the footage they had just shot. While none of them had seen or felt anything while on the bridge, they did think they saw something strange on the footage.

"I'll have to take it back to the house and put it on a larger screen to tell for sure," said Juan.

A portrait reported to be of Alice on her first
day of school (circa 1903).

Everyone agreed.

Next, they agreed to head to Spring Grove Cemetery. But by the time they got there, the gate was locked and the snow was coming down more heavily. The ride to Juan's was slow, but the group was excited about the night's events. They decided to review the film footage at Juan's house immediately.

Once at the house, the group pulled up chairs around Juan's computer.

"I like the large screen you have, Juan; it'll be great for seeing the details," said Minnie.

Juan replied, "Yeah, I'm a gamer."

Juan had the camera footage uploaded quickly, and the group leaned in to watch the screen. A heavy tension began to settle over the room. The anticipation was nearly unbearable. As the footage rolled, the group made notes to themselves about different aspects of what they saw.

Mick asked, "How long is the footage?"

Juan replied, "We have just over twenty minutes here."

Rosa and Jenny made comments as to how cute Minnie looked while conducting the segment. Ron agreed and he and Minnie kissed to the faux disgust of the rest of the group.

Then, at the 7:37 p.m. time mark, a diaphanous figure began to appear behind Minnie. In less than thirty seconds the figure was fully formed and looming over Minnie's left shoulder. It was clearly the ghostly figure of a little girl with golden yellow hair of about twelve years in age. She was wearing what Jenny would later describe as a "mourning dress," the type of outfit a little girl in the late 1800s would have been buried in: a long, flowing white dress. The group of amateur paranormal investigators was enthralled with their results. High-fives were had all around the room as the group basked in its success. They had captured a ghost on film, and they were going to be legends among their fellow classmates.

"Quick!" Mick shouted suddenly. "Let's hear the audio!" Yes, yes! The group chimed in. Ron and Juan set up the recorder and Juan ran it through the speakers. The group listened intently for several long minutes. They could hear themselves talking, Minnie giving her interview and the wind blowing. A car horn could be heard blaring off in the distance. Several minutes in Mick remarked that there wasn't anything strange on the recording so far, but just then, an odd tone came through the speakers. An eerie flexing sound welled up and began to sort of howl. It sounded like an animal that was locked in a cage and wanted out. The strange noises were at first indecipherable. Soon, though, the audio leveled out and what had been noises were beginning to sound like a human voice. The sound was becoming more and more human, but it still sounded as if it were recorded in some strangely shaped room with no baffling. It echoed off an odd chamber. They soon realized that the voice was that of a little girl. Could it be

Alice? It must be Alice, no other ghost was known to haunt that bridge. The ghost of Alice was speaking to them from beyond the grave!

They all leaned in and listened carefully to the voice on the audio. It resonated in strange waves, but was coming into clarity. They could hear Alice, but were still unable to make out exactly what she was saying. The group decided they really needed to get to the Spring Grove Cemetery to see if they could raise her again. The next afternoon, equipment ready, the group of paranormal investigators headed to the Spring Grove Cemetery. They searched around for a while in the snow looking for the grave, only having a description of it, but no lot number. Eventually, they found the grave on a slight hill just up from one of the roads. Ron and Mick found it first, and then the others agreed that they had only found the grave for one very odd reason. While the rest of Spring Grove Cemetery was covered in about eight inches of snow, Alice's headstone, and the ground immediately around it, was free of snow. Why was this, they asked each other. Rosa then looked around and noticed that the panoramic view of Spring Grove from Alice's grave was really quite spectacular.

"All right, everyone," said Juan, "let's get to work."

Juan started the camera rolling, Ron turned on the audio, and Minnie gave an introduction explaining why they were there. In her monologue, Minnie laid out the backstory of Alice and stated that they were at her grave. She then noted the lack of snow around the headstone. Minnie went on to state that they were there to see if they could raise Alice and get her to tell them her story. When Minnie had finished her monologue, the group came together around the headstone. They held hands and Mick led them in a necromantic ritual, a series of chants for raising the spirits of the dead.

> I call forth the spirit of John Dee, that he may be our guide into a world beyond worlds…to the place of the dead!
> I call forth the spirit of John Dee, that his wisdom and power over the grave shall lead us to a young girl known only as Alice, resting here in body for all eternity while her spirit roams free. For it is not her body we seek to raise from slumber, but to know her ever-awakened spirit!
> I call forth . . .

But just as Mick was conjuring a guide to aid in locating the spirit of Alice, a ghostly figure interrupted the ritual and slowly began to appear before them. The diaphanous shape of a young girl in a short blue dress with ruffles around the hem leered beyond them, as if she were looking through them. She had short dark hair and the most haunted eyes. The six friends stood in awe at the ghostly girl standing alongside them. She displayed a sardonic smile. Mick stepped closer to the ghostly girl first. Minnie cringed and Rosa turned her head away. She appeared to be about fourteen or fifteen years old, just a couple years younger than they were.

This was not the girl that appeared to them on the bridge. This was not Alice; or was it? None of the six knew for sure. Had they wrongly assumed that the girl on the bridge was Alice? Was this Alice or some other girl standing before the group? Which ghost was Alice? Was either one Alice?

Confusion raced through the minds of the six friends. They wondered each to themselves: What should we do now? Then they wondered it aloud.

Mick was the first to speak to the dark-haired ghost. "We are listening, spirit," said Mick.

The other five were unable to utter a word. A cold chill ran up Ron's back as he stared at the ghostly figure.

The ghostly spirit breathed out a harsh sound, the sound of a hard "H," the sound of "H" as in *horror* or *hollow*! The winter wind swirled around the group as they cowered in fear at what they had brought to fruition.

Rosa, concerned for the safety of her boyfriend Juan, wrapped her coat around him as he filmed.

Jenny asked, "Are we all seeing a ghost?"

"Yes!" the group collectively replied.

Ron fumbled with the audio equipment.

The ghost finally became audible to the group. She said her name was Jane, a shock to the paranormal investigation group.

Minnie looked over at Jenny and said, "Jane! I thought we were conjuring Alice?"

Jenny just shrugged in amazement.

Mick defended his necromantic ritual adroitness by stating that the ghostly world can be unpredictable even to the professionals, much less an amateur like himself.

"What do we do now?" Ron asked at last.

Minnie answered, "See what she wants."

Still in shock, they all agreed. They turned back to the ghost that was standing before them.

Mick asked the ghostly girl what it was that she wanted.

The girl replied that she wanted to rest in peace.

"What will give you peace; what can we do for you?" asked Rosa.

The ghostly little girl then tasked them with a strange and infinitely more challenging task: find her murderer!

With that, the ghostly girl with the dark hair disappeared into the icy mist of the ambient winter air.

Just then the snow began to fall more heavily. The group decided they would get in out of the cold. Juan invited them over to his house where they could regroup. Once there, they first reviewed the footage they had just shot. Ron and Minnie huddled up close together on the couch while Juan, Rosa, Mick, and Jenny began to lay out plans for how to proceed.

Juan did a quick internet search for a little girl with dark hair and a blue dress in the area around Spring Grove Cemetery. His search yielded a surprising result. They learned the ghost was a murder victim from the 1920s whose killer had never been caught.

In the spring of 1922, the melting snow revealed to the authorities the corpse of a young girl named Jane Goldstein. It seemed that her name had been sewn into the collar of her dress. The Star of David bracelet she wore on her right wrist told the police that she was Jewish. But, when they went to the local rabbis and asked if any of their congregants were missing, they all insisted that the answer was no. The local police knew that the Jews liked to keep to themselves, but surely they would have reported something so important.

The ghost, long dead, wanted the group to find and reveal the killer to the world. The group decided to investigate the murder through public records, newspaper accounts, and police files. Mick said that his family had been Jewish back in Russia and that he felt comfortable speaking with a couple of rabbis to see if he could turn up anything.

Over the next several days the group spent hours and hours investigating the case of Jane Goldstein. Mrs. Albarini found it all very exciting and agreed to let Jenny out of some of her afternoon chores as long as she did her homework. Rosa's parents were not quite so magnanimous; they wanted their daughter to do her homework and her chores. Juan's parents tolerated it all pretty well, figuring that it was a great way to develop some interesting skills. Meanwhile, Minnie's mother and father just wanted her to be home in time for supper. Ron's father let him, more or less, do what he wanted. Ron quipped, "My dad says he raised me right, and he trusts me to make good choices ... as long as I keep my grades up."

The group continued to be reasonably responsible high-schoolers while assiduously researching the case of Jane Goldstein. Mick talked to several rabbis, while the other five went over the internet with a fine-toothed comb. Juan and Rosa spent a couple afternoons going through records at the library. Eventually, a story began to emerge—and what a strange story it was.

It came to light that Jane was thought to have been murdered by the father of a boy named Elyon. She was the daughter of one of the rabbis at the time, and Elyon and Jane were childhood friends. They grew up together in the synagogue, and it was thought that they would be married one day. Elyon's family was wealthy, and they liked the idea that their son was going to marry the rabbi's daughter.

But, as Jane grew into adolescence, she fell in love with another boy. She told Elyon that they could still be friends, but that she was in love with John Tipton. He would just have to get over her, she'd told him in no uncertain terms.

Elyon raged, "But he's a goy! How could you betray me ... or your father, the rabbi ... for a goy!" In his rage, he went to tell his father about the breakup and the goy [non-Jewish person]. Elyon's father had been plotting the marriage to bolster his family's standing in the community. He was just as upset as Elyon, as this meant an insult to his family name.

The next bit of information that the paranormal investigation team was able to unearth was a newspaper clipping from the day after the body was found. They had a lot of information about the autopsy and Jane Goldstein's subsequent burial in Clifton Cemetery, but none on the murder or who was responsible. The group decided they needed to visit Clifton Cemetery.

They eventually found the grave of Jane Goldstein, and set out to see if they could raise her. They did not know if they needed to be Jewish for this or if their usual methods would work. Mick said that though neither he nor his parents was really Jewish, maybe because his grandparents had been he was best suited to try to contact Jane. He proceeded to fumble through some Hebrew, as best he could remember, the prayer his grandmother used to sing to his mother when she was a child. Before long, the ghost of Jane was once again standing beside them.

From the ghost of Jane they learned that she had been murdered by Elyon's father, who was angry with her for breaking up with his son and, therefore, putting a shanda [disgrace] on his family.

Elyon's father saw Jane walking alone one evening near the park. He waved pleasantly at her, and when she, unaware of the father's rage, came over to talk with him, he grabbed her and pulled her behind some buildings into an alley. The strong man easily overpowered the young girl, and soon she was struggling for her life. Jane's ghost recalled how Elyon's father raged, "A *shanda fur die goy*!" as he brutally strangled her. She also recalled how the father cleaned up the scene where he had killed her and then dumped her body out in the snow near the Ohio River under the cover of darkness. Fortunately for the father, and unfortunately for Jane, no one had seen the murder.

Mick said, "Well, the father will never be punished in this life, but we know who he is and his crime has been exposed. We'll take our story to the rabbis and they, too, will know about his crime. A conviction by reputation, I'd say. A real *shanda*." The group looked back over at Jane and thanked her for revealing her story to them.

With her story told, Jane's appearance began to change. She slowly began to get a soft white glow around her, rather than the harsh light she had previously shown. Soon, she vanished into the winter air. The group felt a relieved peaceful calm descend on them.

Juan caught the whole story on film. It was not the kind of evidence that would stand up in court, but it was good enough for the paranormal investigation team. They had their murderer, and they had a complete story from beginning to end.

"Pride," said Mick. "It was all about pride . . . isn't that one of the seven deadly sins in the Catholic tradition?"

Juan and Rosa answered, "Yes, it is."

The others were at a near loss for words over their investigation.

"Well, I, for one, can't wait to get back to the house and review all this footage, write this up, and present it to the world," Ron stated.

Jenny and Minnie agreed.

They packed up the camera and recording equipment, and when they were done, they turned to head back to the car.

Then . . . standing before them was the nearly translucent ghost of Alice . . .

CHAPTER TWELVE

St. John German Catholic Cemetery

An Unsettled Haunting

This lugubrious looking mansion overlooks St. John German Catholic Cemetery. It is where George Swettol resided before his untimely demise. Those living in the house in recent years claim to hear him within its walls.

St. John German Catholic Cemetery, where George Swettol met his terrifying fate. Some say his bloody residue can still be seen today.

Parapsychologists generally agree that if a person is mentally or emotionally disturbed at the moment of death, their soul cannot attain rest, that it is trapped between the two planes of existence in an unsettled state. This unsettled state can manifest itself in many ways. A spirit can be trapped within a certain structure; i.e., a house or building. It can be trapped in a space, such as a park, cemetery, or a city. In some cases the spirit is trapped in a time warp, appearing and disappearing at what seems to the living to be random times. Professional parapsychologists have various views on what causes this, and no two cases are exactly alike. Being deceased, a fraction of the spirit is on the other side of the curtain, in a boundless eternity. Most of these spirits are eventually laid to rest through prayer, forgiveness, or some other type of resolution.

Some, however, remain in a suspended state indefinitely. This was what happened to a man named George Swettol. This is his story.

George had never been, from the time he was a child, a calm person. As a child he was called "hyper" by his parents. His teachers called him "precocious"; they could not, no matter what they tried, get George under control. George's brother and sister, Randall and Linda, were very average children in their temperament and behavior. The other children at his school did not want to be friends with such a "difficult" classmate, and George found himself isolated quite often. The teachers at his school did not know what to make of him. He eventually quit school and began taking odd jobs around Cincinnati. The police arrested him for petty things a few times over the years, but he never served any real time in jail.

He drifted from job to job, neighborhood to neighborhood, never settling anywhere for more than a few months. He was married for a short time back in the early 'sixties, but his wife left him over his inability to keep a job. George had no friends and nothing to call an anchor. Both his brother and his sister reached out to him and offered him help from time to time, but he seemed unable, or unwilling, to take them up on it. One could tell right away upon meeting him that he was highly intelligent, highly emotional, and yet, a fractured man. He carried around with him a sense of sadness and desperation. Like many men of his generation, George smoked and drank heavily.

In early 1969, George's parents met with him to see if there was something to be done about his life. His parents agreed that the political, economic, and social turmoil of the past decade had done little to assuage George's sense of instability. George himself could offer no explanation for his erratic and unstable lifestyle. His parents suggested they buy him a small house in Hamilton so he could get away from the frantic city life in Cincinnati. He rejected this idea before walking out the door. It was four years before his parents saw him again.

One hazy morning in the early fall of 1978, George woke up lying among the gravestones of St. John German Catholic Cemetery. His head hurt, and he wondered how he had gotten there. His clothes were wet, and he felt the pangs of hunger run through his frail frame. He looked down only to see an empty bottle of Kentucky bourbon at his feet. He soon realized that he had spent the prior night drinking in the graveyard. Feeling sick and angry and somewhat drunk, George looked around as the gravestones sloshed back and forth in front of him. He had soiled himself and was becoming ashamed of his state of being.

The sun was nearly up before George got himself on his feet and walking around. The graveyard was empty of people and noise. The neighborhood was quiet—as quiet as a funeral parlor after the last guest was gone. He staggered slowly home to his attic apartment across the street from the cemetery. The long stairway up to his room was daunting to a man in his condition. A letter from his sister awaited him upon his arrival. In it, she offered to help him in any way she could. The letter ended with her expressing how worried she was about him. Once in his room, he showered, changed clothes, and fell back asleep on the couch. When he woke up again a couple hours later, he still felt horrible and decided a drink would solve his ills; the next thing he knew he was drinking in the cemetery again. He was alone as usual, muttering to himself how those buried around him were the lucky ones.

The sky that day was cloudy. An ominous darkness fell over the cemetery and settled around the tombs. A late summer storm was rolling into Cincinnati by mid-afternoon, but George was, by then, too drunk to notice. The sky grew dark and the winds howled like wolves. Lightning broke on the edges of the clouds, and the quartz in the gravestones glistened like diamonds in the flashes of light. The rain beat down like an insane pianist pounding out his masterpiece of madness. The hours of the clock crept by as slowly as the clouds, but eventually they moved into the past.

The next morning, the sun's warm rays were breaking on the tranquil eastern horizon when the superintendent arrived to open the cemetery gates. As he did every morning, he walked the grounds to check on the property. What he found that morning, he's never likely to forget. At first, all things looked normal, but then, thirteen rows in, he saw the contorted corpse of George Swettol lying beside one of the headstones. The superintendent walked back to the office to call the police, while thinking to himself how ironic it was that he should find a corpse in a graveyard. At the conclusion of a short investigation, the police ruled it "death by misadventure." He had fallen over a foot marker and hit his head on a gravestone. The wound on his head matched perfectly the bloodstains at the edge of the gravestone. Alcohol thins the blood, and he had bled to death on the ground.

Although George Swettol's body was buried elsewhere, his apparition remains in St. John German Catholic Cemetery to this day. Many visitors over these decades have reported sensing or seeing an eerie orb hovering ominously among the stones. He was restless in life, and his ghost remains restless in the afterlife as well.

Local legend says that for one night each year, in September, George Swettol's blood appears on the gravestone where he hit his head…no doubt, the spiritual residue of an unsettled haunting.

CHAPTER THIRTEEN

St. John German Catholic Cemetery

Caparra

This Gothic-looking mansion near Hyde Park is believed to be the site of Caparra's final crime.

Caparra was a thief. He had, though, not always been a thief. Ever since he was a young boy he had been attracted to the thrill of gangster legends—stories from the old West and tales of danger and excitement. He would spend the endless hours of summer listening to an old man at the corner store spin yarns of Jesse James, Soapy Smith, James Hind, and other highwaymen. He waited with anticipation for the latest Penny Dreadful to arrive so he could read the stories of vampires, serial killers, and supernatural shenanigans. His older brother, Dario, would read him stories by Edgar Allen Poe and H. G. Wells. From his earliest years, Caparra could dream of nothing more exciting than an adventure of his own.

Caparra was raised in a strict religious family who let him have his stories, as long as he understood the difference between right and wrong, legend and reality. He was raised with an education and a set of skills that would serve him well in the business world.

By the time the young Caparra had grown into his late teens and early twenties, he was becoming quite the gentleman. He was making progress on what promised to be a long and successful career in business. He dressed well and was starting to be recognized by the leading figures of the day. A degree in business from the University of Cincinnati helped Caparra gain acclaim in the business circles of society.

However, things began to change for young Caparra in the spring of 1909. It was then that he took a fancy to a young woman named Amanda. She was beautiful, poised, and a little bit mysterious. Caparra loved Amanda, and Amanda loved absinthe and opium. So, Caparra began to drink with Amanda. Over the holidays of 1909, he and Amanda spent every minute they could together. As the winter of 1909 came to an end, Caparra began to think about proposing to her. They continued to drink and indulge in opium together. Business acquaintances began to note his increasingly erratic behavior during those months. He would often nod off during business meetings, or not attend at all.

Things really began to go wrong for Caparra one afternoon in the early summer. That fateful day, he found Amanda dead. When he found her, she was covered in her own vomit, with skin as pale gray as the color of a gravestone. She had overdosed on a toxic cocktail of drink and drug. The post-mortem stated that she also had some mysterious burn marks in the small of her back. Marks she could not have inflicted on herself. The suspicious eye of the police came on Caparra. In his grief, Caparra drowned himself in bourbon. He soon found himself on the outs with many in the business community, due to his excessive drinking and inappropriate behavior. In a matter of weeks, he had gone from a promising young man to the margins of Cincinnati society. Drink and opium had completely taken over his life. His mind became a patchwork of desperation and grief. Still, those legends of crime stories remained in his thoughts. He felt more drawn to them than ever, because now he knew what it was like to be one of them: the lonely criminal against the world. A childhood dream of crime and adventure was about to befall Caparra in ways even he could not have imagined.

Caparra had always been able to lead a good life while admiring the legends of crime; but here he was, huddled behind some shrubs on the verge of robbing a large home. Perhaps it was a fledgling robber's first attempt at an emerging career. As he waited for the family to leave their house to attend church, he pondered over what had brought him to a life of crime in reality. Opium and absinthe had been responsible for his downfall, and he was desperate for money to buy his next drink and stash of drugs.

His thoughts turned back to the crime at hand when a large four-horse carriage came around from behind the house. It stopped at the front door and picked up the family: father, mother, and children. The family's butler climbed up top to join the coachman. From behind the shrubs, Caparra watched as the carriage slowly turned at the corner and disappeared into the streets of the city. The family was gone to church for over two hours, he thought, plenty of time to ransack the home. A wave of opium-induced sensations came over him as he started to make his way to the house.

Like a snake slithering through the tall summer grass, he made his way up onto the side porch and slipped in through an open window. The quiet in the house was almost deafening. He first looked around himself at the rather large rooms decorated in the late Victorian style of the day. Long curtains framed the floor-to-ceiling windows, expansive rugs covered hardwood floors. The furniture was almost all imported from Europe, with the exception of a few handcrafted pieces from New England. Oversized portraits of the homeowner's ancestors hung on the wallpapered and wainscoted walls. The silver sconces and candelabras gave the rooms a classy finished touch. Caparra was used to a fine home, but this was extraordinary even by his standards. He began to rifle through the furniture drawers. Pull after pull revealed all sorts of treasures. He found silverware, place settings, pocket watches, knives, and bullets. In almost every drawer he found coins and currency from around the world.

He caught his breath and began to make his way up the grand stairway to the second floor. Before him were six large and heavy wooden doors of the finest craftsmanship. As he entered the first room a rush came over him. He had entered what he supposed was the daughter's bedroom. A neatly made brass bed and a large mirrored nightstand sat before him. He began to go through the drawers in the bedroom only to find the most ordinary things: combs, perfumes, and ribbons. The only thing of value he found in the dresser was a pearl bracelet and matching necklace. A few low-value coins were hidden in a gold talcum powder box. He then searched through the armoire but found there only clothes and hats. A few toys were scattered about on the floor.

Caparra then moved on to the next room. There he found a similar arrangement and nothing of any real worth to him in a material sense. This bedroom, too, belonged to a daughter, but she seemed to be somewhat older than the first child, based on her belongings. The dolls on the bed were arranged neatly and orderly, as if the older girl had positioned them there. The only thing he found of value in this room was a well-worn diary. He did not have time to read it then, but diaries can be invaluable if one were to ever want to blackmail someone. Oh, the secrets they hide from the eyes and ears of a gossiping city. He slipped the diary into his pocket for later reading. Caparra then left the room and headed back into the hallway.

The third room proved to be of much more interest. This, it turned out, was the master bedroom. The room was massive. It contained a private bathroom, reading suite, and two closets, something Caparra had never seen before. The wallpaper was similar to that he had noted downstairs, imported from Europe. He felt for a moment like he was in a museum and not someone's private home. Fancy new gas lights lit the room brilliantly but cast unnerving shadows across the floor. He started to again go through the belongings. First the drawers on the dresser. There he found more currency, a pistol, a pair of gold cufflinks, a silver and sapphire ascot pin, and some other knickknacks. A small chest with an extraordinary inlayed pattern sitting beside the dresser next caught Caparra's attention.

He bent down over the wooden chest and began to open it, but just as he did he heard a noise behind him. A frightened Caparra spun around only to see the vastness of the empty room before him. A sigh of relief passed through his lips. He turned back to the chest and again began to open it, but once again he heard a noise from behind. He flung himself around to see the father standing in front of him. He was not at church after all, but had returned to the house. Caparra's eyes grew wide. The father, a tall strong-looking man, raised a pistol and pointed it at Caparra. He flinched for only a second before regaining his composure. The man had not shot him outright, and so maybe he had a chance to negotiate himself out of this situation or just escape unharmed. He had not actually stolen anything yet, and maybe if he just left the father would figure no harm done. At that second, though, he remembered the pistol he had just seen in the drawer. He asked himself if it was the one the father was pointing at him, or if the pistol he'd seen was still in the drawer. This question he could not ask or answer. He bided his time.

The two men just starred at each other for what to Caparra seemed like an eternity. Beads of sweat began to form on his forehead and run down behind his glasses. The father remained as cool as an onion in the darkness of a root cellar. His cold, dark eyes just continued to stare silently at Caparra.

At length, Caparra began to speak. To talk his way out of the situation. The father just continued to stare while Caparra rambled on and on about his reasons for the invasion. The high of the opium and the adrenaline of the break-in had worn off and Caparra found himself standing in the stark naked light of reality. All his pain and fear was quickly welling to the surface. Soon though, Caparra realized that the father was not going to negotiate or just let him walk out. He wished he had taken a moment to read the diary, so that he might have some starting point at which to make his case.

Suddenly, the father cocked the hammer on the pistol. The familiar sound of metal scraping metal sent shockwaves of fear through Caparra as he realized he might be on the verge of death. For a flash, the memory of Amanda went through his mind and the idea of joining her on the other side seemed palatable. But his instinct for survival brought him back to his senses. Several more long minutes painfully passed between the two men involved in the standoff. From the downstairs hallway, the sound of the clock striking noon could be heard reverberating throughout the house. Caparra knew his time was ticking away.

Then, just as suddenly as he appeared, the father jumped towards Caparra, catching him by surprise. The two men slammed against the wooden dresser hard enough to knock both of them to the ground. The father held his grip on the pistol as Caparra tried his best to grab it. He locked his strong hands around the father's wrist to hold the pistol away from himself. With his free hand, Caparra began to punch the father in the ribs. The father groaned in pain as he exhaled. Fists flew in fury as each man wrestled for control of the pistol. First Caparra got in a good hit with his knee, and then the father returned the favor with a powerful left hook to Caparra's jaw.

After an especially hard hit, Caparra's spectacles flew from his face and bounced across the floor before landing under the bed. The cat that was hiding there hissed in disdain at the intrusion of the glasses into his hiding spot. Both men continued to tussle with each other as only two desperate fighters can. They each had a lot to lose. The young man at last grabbed the father's lapel with his free hand and slammed him against the edge of the bedroom door. When he pulled the father away, even without his glasses, he could tell that there was blood rolling down the wood paneled door. The father then pulled Caparra down hard into some books that were neatly stacked beside a chair. The books scattered. After several more minutes of thrashing each other about the bedroom, they spilled out into the hallway. Caparra could not seem to wrestle the pistol away from the determined father. In a moment of lucidity, Caparra wondered what control the man must have for him to have not fired a single shot during the tornado of a fight.

Soon, the father grabbed Caparra by the back of his jacket and in one swift motion, threw him down the stairs. As Caparra tumbled, Amanda's memory spun around inside his head like the motion of a Ferris wheel careening out of control. He reached out to grasp the handrail in a futile effort to balance himself

Caparra was ultimately buried in St. John German Catholic Cemetery.

and break his fall. Each impact he made against the stairs hurt just a little more than the prior one. Stability eluded him as he fell. As he rapidly descended the stairway, the diary that had been in his jacket pocket flipped out and landed on the eighth stair from the bottom. Just as the diary was landing, Caparra was crashing down against the hardwood floor.

A few seconds later, when he awoke from his unconsciousness, Caparra saw the father standing over him pointing the gun right between his eyes. A cold stare radiated from the slightly out-of-focus face that sat like a full moon hovering over the barrel of the pistol. Caparra swallowed hard. He tried to keep his lips still as he exhaled as quietly as he could. One wrong move and the father was going to fire a bullet into his head. Thoughts about what to do next raced through Caparra's mind. Should he beg for mercy? Should he continue to fight, or should he just let the man shoot him now. At length, he decided.

He suddenly jerked his arm to distract the father; and when the father glanced at his arm, Caparra wretched his legs hard, knocking the father to the floor. The pistol the father was holding flew across the room. It first hit the soft cushions of the sofa before bouncing off and clattering across the floor. It came to rest under a chair beside the grandfather clock.

They were finally on an even footing. Caparra lunged forward and grabbed the father by the lapels, heaving him up off the floor. The two men tussled into the large living room. Caparra could feel some blood rolling down his left leg where he had slammed it against the corner of the mahogany desk. The wound pulsed in pain. He spun the father several times around to disorient him before shoving him backwards against the oversized stone fireplace. The father's head slammed hard against the fireplace. He rolled his eyes upwards and slumped to the ground. Blood soon began to roll out from under his head and across the rug before finally seeping into the cracks of the hardwood floor. Caparra stood over him for several long minutes, but the man lay still. Caparra punched the man to see if he could get him to move, but the man remained as still as a corpse. No pulse could be detected when Caparra put his fingers to the man's throat. He stood up, pulled at his chin and thought to himself, "I've just killed a man. I'm a murderer. I've never killed anyone before . . . what do I do now?" His mind swirled in a frantic spin.

Panic began to settle into Caparra's mind. What should he do? Run? Finish the burglary? What good would it do to run now?

He looked back over at the unmoving body that lay before him. Caparra decided the best thing to do was finish the burglary quickly. He reasoned that he might as well get something out of being a murderer. An eerie silence came over the house as the feeling of death crept around every corner. As he continued to roam around the house Caparra felt like he was being followed. He knew for sure that the ghost of the man he had just killed was there with him. As he looked around the house, he felt a bit of guilt as well as a feeling of jealousy at the fine home he was unjustifiably in. After several minutes of checking to see if anyone was around, he was satisfied that there had been no witnesses. He arduously went back upstairs, as a dank haze shrouded his mind.

Once he was in the master bedroom, he again began to rifle through the family's possessions. He returned to the small wooden chest where his nightmare had begun. As he stared, like the unflinching eye of the midday sun, at the contents of the chest, he was in awe. A startling sound elsewhere in the house drew his attention momentarily, but then he remembered the cat under the bed. He turned back to the chest. Oh the treasure that sat before him. He thought to himself if he could just get out of the house with this one thing he would be set for life. He could move away from wretched Cincinnati, from himself, and start all over again. He started to reach down into the chest, but all of a sudden he felt a cold breeze pour over his shoulder and around his neck. His eyes grew wide with fear as he spun around to see the ghostly figure of a man standing there.

"The ghost of the father!" he thought to himself. "The ghost of the father that I just killed has come back to haunt me . . . Oh, please have mercy on me!" The ghostly figure just continued to stare at Caparra. He began to sense something strange. An odd feeling began to take over Caparra. The ghost was not the father, but something else. If it wasn't the ghost of the father . . . then who was it?

"Who are you? What do you want of me?" asked Caparra.

The ghost explained that he was Caparra's better half—the part of him that could have chosen to be a good person, the part that realized there was still time to do the right thing.

"But I'm a murderer; I'm half a ghost myself already!" screamed Caparra. The ghost replied that it was true that half of him had died that day, the half of him that was innocent and pure, untouched by an irrevocable sin. The ghost explained that until today, any injustice he had committed could be easily rectified with an apology, but today he had crossed a line that no man has ever come back from. Caparra made a few more lame excuses before bending down in acquiescence to his better self.

"What can I do to set things right?" he asked the ghostly figure.

Just then, before he could receive an answer, the silence was broken. Caparra heard the carriage pull up in front of the house. The ghostly figure vanished into the vastness of the room. Caparra regained his composure. He moved quickly down the stairs with stealth and into the living room. He moved up next to the father's body, standing over it, and awaited the arrival of the family.

Caparra heard the front door open. He heard the butler say how good it was to be back home. The children came scampering in and dispersed about the house. Their mother called to them, "Children, lunch will be served in half an hour." The wife then came around the corner, only to look shocked at seeing

Caparra standing over the body of her husband. Her eyes widened. The butler suddenly appeared behind her, looking over her shoulder at the horrible sight. He glanced around to see if the children were anywhere in sight before stepping out in front of the wife and demanding an explanation from Caparra.

"Say man, what has happened here?" demanded the butler. Caparra looked up and said, "Ma'am, I have murdered your husband; you should get the police. I was robbing you, and he came upon me. They will want my life for what I have done, and they deserve to have it."

The wife ran out the front door and screamed at the top of her lungs, "MURDER!"

All the neighbors came running, as well as the policeman who had been standing on the corner. Caparra remained in a paralyzed state over the body. The cop immediately put the cuffs on Caparra and led him outside as the paddy wagon arrived. Caparra was taken to a musty, dank jail cell to await questioning from the authorities. An investigation ensued. The widow and the children were vigorously questioned. The scene was gone over and a rather lengthy report was written. Caparra was questioned down at the station before being locked away in a holding cell again.

In the midst of the investigation, the police chief said to the detective, "I want this one done by the book; they are a prominent family, and I'm thinking about running for Mayor next election. Wrapping up a big case will help me say that I'm tough on crime."

"Yes sir," replied the police detective.

In the days that followed, Caparra was subsequently booked for murder. The days and nights passed slowly as he waited for trial. In the meantime, the widow of the father was nearly inconsolable. She cried anytime anyone asked about her late husband.

During the investigation, a large kitchen knife was found in the fireplace. The fire had burned away any blood or fingerprints, but the knife matched the wounds on the deceased's body. This evidence was sealed until trial.

During the trial, as Caparra was getting ready to plead guilty, the piece of odd evidence about the knife was brought against him. The coroner's post-mortem report stated that the father had died of three knife stabs to the heart. He did have a small cut to the back of his head but that would not have been sufficient to cause his death.

The coroner's report conflicted with what Caparra did, or so he thought. The lawyer for Caparra urged his client to not plead guilty on the stand, but to hear what this new piece of evidence was all about. He explained to his lawyer that he had shoved the father into the mantle, causing the cut on the back of his head; but that was all. When the father passed out from the head cut, he left him alone after that, sure that the man was dead. He stated he did nothing more to the man. He swore he had no knife, that he had never stabbed the man. Someone else must have come along after that and stabbed the father. Strangely, though the scene of the crime did not show it, the lawyer believed Caparra when he said he had never stabbed the man.

The jury, though, did not believe Caparra. They thought his "secondary killer" theory was implausible. Both the widow and the butler testified that they had found Caparra standing over the dead body. He was quickly found guilty of murder and sentenced to death by a newly adopted method of execution: the electric chair.

He appealed the verdict, arguing that he had only injured the victim and that the person who had stabbed the father was still on the loose. His appeal was quickly turned down. One month later, a priest was called in to read last rites to Leo Caparra before he was executed for murder in the course of a crime.

The priest listened carefully to Caparra as he pleaded with him to listen to his story. The priest listened to Caparra's confession of drinking, philandering, assault, and robbery. Caparra begged the priest to believe that he had not committed murder, that he had not stabbed the man. In just under an hour, Caparra told the priest everything and begged forgiveness. The priest said he believed Caparra. He stated that he had presided over many confessions, and he could tell a lie from the truth in his sleep. Then, an officer led the priest out. The priest went straight to the judge and asked for some time. The judge gave the priest one day to find any new evidence. If he could find none, Caparra would be executed the next afternoon.

The priest went to the house and introduced himself to the butler as Father Bleiben. The butler kindly introduced himself as Gabriel Widersprechen in reply. The priest cast a curious look into Gabriel's eyes. "Widersprechen you say? What an odd name . . ." To which Gabriel replied, "I must contradict your assertion." Both men broke out laughing at their play on words.

"All joking aside, tell me a bit about this case. We are just about to bury a man whom some say may be innocent." said the priest.

"A sad case indeed, Father," said Gabriel. "My lady and the children came home from church, only to find the condemned lurking over the body with a knife in his hand. As soon as he saw us, he threw the knife into the fireplace. Father, I saw the scene myself; he was not an innocent man. My employer's head was cut a bit, but that wound was small. He was stabbed to death, and three times did the knife enter his nefarious heart." Gabriel continued. "As for my lady, she has been in a constant state of mourning since that day. Say, Father, what makes people say that Caparra was innocent?"

"Just his word," replied the priest. He leaned in close to Gabriel and looked him square in the eye; "and I know he was telling the truth. Leo Caparra only knocked out your master . . . and you know it too."

Gabriel swallowed hard. "I do?" he said.

Chapter Thirteen: St. John German Catholic Cemetery Caparra

"You know it . . . because you are the one who stabbed him with a knife from the kitchen! You know it because you saw the whole thing unfold from the kitchen door. You saw Caparra push him into the fireplace encasement, you saw him slump to the floor, and you then saw Caparra go back upstairs. When Caparra was out of sight, you went to check on your master, finding him unconscious, wounded slightly. You recognized that this was your opportunity to murder your master and place the blame on a burglar. I suspect you had been looking for that opportunity for quite a while, and you took it as soon as it presented itself. Oh, how perfect it almost was. Your lady with the children at church as their alibi. Sunday, your day off to attend church yourself. On a normal Sunday, you would have been at church, too, but you were not. I saw you and the family arrive at church that morning. After Bible study, I saw the father leave. I saw you follow him. I later noticed that only the wife and the children were in the pews. I noticed, too, that the lady looked quite nervous, glancing around as if she were looking for something. At the time, I thought that she was looking for her husband, but later I realized that she was looking for you. You followed the husband home, hoping to get him alone. It was just serendipity on your part that Caparra was in the house. Your intention was to murder the husband and then slip back to church, providing yourself with an alibi, but when you came upon the burglar, you had your escape plan; you

The site in St. John's German Catholic Cemetery
where the priest heard a most bizarre confession.

would simply blame it on the intruder. And why not? Who would believe him anyway? He was a burglar. Perfect. Nearly perfect."

"Father, that is quite an accusation!" said Gabriel defiantly.

"An accusation that is true," replied Father Bleiben.

Gabriel stared coldly at the priest before he broke down. "All right, Father; I did it. But how did you know?"

The Priest replied that between what he had observed at the church that morning and Caparra's confession, he had all he needed to believe in Caparra's innocence. The priest also reminded Widersprechen that he had referred to his employer as "nefarious," a derogatory term indicating a thinly veiled hatred. Father Bleiben grinned. "But none of that matters now, though, for you have confessed to me, and we are not in the confessional booth."

Gabriel flashed an angry look at Father Bleiben.

"Tell me, what reason did you have to kill your employer? He paid you well and treated you well. What possible reason did you have to kill him? Was it over your affections for the lady of the house?" asked the father.

Gabriel looked startled. He turned to face the father, "You know of that, too?"

Father Bleiben put his right index finger in the air and stated, "My son, a priest is the eyes and ears of God. A priest watches over his flock. He also hears the confessions of those who feel the guilt of sin."

"I guess you are going to turn me in to the police now?" said Gabriel quietly.

"No, my son; you are," said the priest.

Gabriel lowered his head.

A few weeks later, Leo Caparra was sentenced to two years in jail for robbery and assault. He had pled guilty and was resigned to his fate. He stated in the press that he was the luckiest man in the world. He stated that he had had the crime adventure of a lifetime, having been almost convicted as a murderer in the course of a crime. He went on to state that from then on he'd leave the crime stories to the *Penny Dreadful*s.

A few days later, another priest conducted confession and absolution rites for Gabriel. The week after that, Gabriel Widersprechen was executed by the state of Ohio for murder. It was a couple days later that Widersprechen was laid to rest in St. John German Catholic Cemetery. Some of those who stroll the cemetery today say that they can feel the presence of a murderer in their midst.

CHAPTER FOURTEEN

St. Mary's Graveyard

(Cincinnati)
The Fleague

John Ridinger's grave, in St. Mary's Catholic Cemetery, is the site of a strange legend.

John Ridinger was a man of modest success in business, married with children. To his family he was a wonderful man. To his dog, a best friend, and to society, a regular kind of guy. All in all, an average man of his generation.

But, according to a legend that developed in the years after his death, John Ridinger held a secret. A strange secret, an anomaly of bizarre proportions. John Ridinger attracted fleas. Not just a few fleas he got from the dog in the heat of summer; no, he attracted a lot of fleas year-round. He attracted enough fleas that one day his children made a joke that he had enough fleas to start his own baseball team. "A league of fleas," they joked. "The Fleague," he would respond in jest, although to him it was really not that funny. But, he needed to keep a brave face so as to not scare the children. Although he joked about it with them, he was really quite concerned. The itching was disconcerting at best and outright maddening at times. The pesky little things attacked him by the hundreds. As The Fleague continued its reign of terror over his nerve endings year after year, it just got worse. He could lie next to his wife in bed writhing in pain and terror, while his wife felt nothing.

John and his wife went to see the priest. Confession was made, counseling was completed, and prayers were said, but still the fleas continued to eat at John.

He thought that he might be cursed or hexed in some way. Had he committed an offence against some malevolent spirit that wanted revenge? A visit to a Tarot card reader brought no answers. An animal medium came to the house to try and contact the spirits of the fleas, but to no avail. His skin pulsed red, inflamed by a thousand bites and endless scratching.

He began to drive himself mad with the notion that he was cursed. "Why else," he would ask himself obsessively, "am I being followed by the fleas?" He bathed regularly, he kept his house clean, he purchased flea powder, he prayed, he even went so far as to get rid of his dog. What else was a man to do?

The fleas would bite and create terrible sensations up and down his arms and legs. He would scratch until his skin was raw and bleeding. He would sit in the pews at church and nervously look around to see if anyone else noticed the fleas. As time went on The Fleague drove him insane. They were all he could talk about. His wife would find him curled up in the corner of the living room madly scratching at the fleas he swore were there. Even when his wife and children swore they could see no fleas, he still felt the creatures crawling on his skin, under his clothes, and in his hairline. Night after night he would lie in bed swatting at the fleas while his wife lay next to him and worried.

Eventually, his family had him committed to a psychiatric ward for evaluation. In the ward he sat quietly and calmly with the doctor. The psychiatrist asked him a lot of questions, and John answered each one of them in a sane, calm, and reasonable manner. Not once during his seventy-two-hour stay did he scratch at the fleas. Not once did he scream in agony at the sensation of tiny insects crawling on him. The doctor noted his response to each question as completely normal. He was released with a clean bill of mental health. The doctor's report stated that the psychiatrists thought that he had simply gotten a few fleas on him from a dog, and that it had upset him. It was, to them, nothing more serious.

John's wife finally convinced him to visit the priest again. They spent several hours in prayer and confession, but John still felt overwhelmed by The Fleague. All he wanted was for the horrible biting sensations to leave him be.

The torture inflicted by the fleas continued. In time he became so engulfed by the fleas that he could not lie down or even sit. Everything was uncomfortable. Sleep was out of the question. He was exhausted to the point of contemplating suicide.

At long length, John Ridinger died of what the doctor described as "heart failure due to high blood pressure brought on by stress." The wife agreed that he had been stressed, even driven to madness, about The Fleague for years. The post-mortem also noted hundreds of scratches and small red welts on his entire body. She confided to the doctor that he thought he was hexed. The doctor said, with a glimmer in his eye, "Well then, death was probably the best thing for him, really." He was buried a few days later.

His children never experienced the strange malady as their father. They did, however, continue to wonder about the mysterious condition they called The Fleague. Was their father really affected by actual fleas, or was he insane with an obsession beyond his control?

John Ridinger was laid to rest in St. Mary's Graveyard a few years ago now. His headstone sits not far from a beautiful weeping willow tree. According to local legend, if you visit the grave of John Ridinger, you may soon feel the tiny insects begin to crawl on your skin. You may start to itch, an itch that is futile to scratch, an itch that may drive you mad if you remain. So if you do visit the grave of John Ridinger, remember you, too, may become a victim of The Fleague.

CHAPTER FIFTEEN

St. Mary's Graveyard

(Cincinnati)
A Sense of Immeasurable Sorrow

St. Mary's Cemetery, where many of the victims from Cincinnati's infamous orphanage fire were laid to rest.

Chapter Fifteen: St. Mary's Graveyard (Cincinnati) A Sense of Immeasurable Sorrow

The story begins in the middle of the nineteenth century, when what's now called "Point of Immeasurable Sorrow" was the site of a Roman Catholic orphanage run by the Sisters of Charity of Cincinnati. The orphanage was the home to several dozen young boys whose parents were either dead or incapacitated in some manner. They were raised by the nuns, and had been since the orphanage had been founded some fifty years earlier. These orphans lived according to the norms of those days: going to school to learn a useful trade, and having a strict regimen of Catholic doctrine. Since this was a Catholic home, some of the older boys would eventually be studying to enter the priesthood. There weren't many options or opportunities back then for those children without parents. It may not have been a happy life filled with joy and fun, but by all accounts, they were having their basic needs met on a daily basis, which for many of them was better than life on the streets—for if they were not in the care of the sisters, they would be in the care of the streets and its wicked ways.

Daily life in the orphanage was filled with mind-numbing routine. Each morning the children were woken to prayers, breakfast, and a long school day. In the afternoons, there were more prayers and occupational training. The evening brought more prayers, dinner, and one hour of storytelling. Nighttime brought more prayers, with lights out by nine. Saturday was a day for quiet activities, such as reading or cleaning. Bathing came every Wednesday and Sunday morning before church services.

When the Civil War broke out, the routine of the orphanage was disrupted. The sisters were asked to become nurses for wounded Union soldiers. While continuing as an orphanage, the large brick facility also served as a temporary hospital. A great number of Union wounded were sent to recuperate there. A doctor was brought in to serve the severely wounded. One of the nuns, Sister Anthony O'Connell, served on the front lines and became known as "The Angel of the Battlefield" for her work with the soldiers. When the war ended in 1865, the facility returned to its regular routine. But the residue of war had left its mark upon the orphanage.

The monotonous schedule at the orphanage came to a tragic end one night in February 1866, when a mysterious fire broke out in the dormitory. The fire spread quickly through the building. The long drapes on the floor-to-ceiling windows were the first things to go up in flames. The rafters above the large rooms were the next to become engulfed. It was too late by the time the children became aware of the smoke and flames that were enveloping them. The fire department was called, but Catholics in those days were not considered a priority, and so there was a long delay in sending a fire brigade. A couple hours later, when the fire department finally arrived, the building had been gutted, reduced to burnt cinder blocks and smoldering rubble. Many of the children and several of the Sisters had burned to death in the flames. The ones who had not been directly killed by the flames had died of smoke inhalation—a most horrible way to perish.

Those who were able to escape lay on the cold damp lawn and watched in dismay as their only friends screamed in terror. An explosion in the boiler room shook the remaining bricks until they crumbled to the ground. Steam swirled off the wet bricks and vanished into the frigid February air like ghosts in the night.

The next day, an investigation was conducted. Though the cause of the fire was never identified, what was discovered haunts the Catholic community to this day. In the smoldering ashes, deep within the bowels of the building, the investigators found a small boy, completely unharmed. Not only was the boy not harmed by the smoke or the flames, he was not even dirty. He was as clean as Sunday morning. He wore a long-sleeved dress shirt covered in a sleeveless sweater and long wool pants. His black leather shoes still shined. One of the assistant investigators took him by the hand, and led him up out of the rubble and into the waiting arms of one of the sisters. The other assistant investigator went to tell the lead investigator that they had found a living boy deep down in the basement and rescued him. A few minutes later the investigator went to speak with the sister to record the particulars of the boy: name, age, and description. When he arrived to speak with her, there was no boy. It seemed he had vanished into thin air, having been seen only by the two assistant investigators who found him. No one else, including the sister, had ever seen such a boy. It has never been established who the boy was, where he came from, or where he went.

In the weeks after that, the victims were buried one by one. The young boys were all buried in St. Mary's Cemetery in north central Cincinnati, along with some of the sisters. Two of the sisters were subsequently buried with their families in St. Mary's Cemetery in Fort Mitchell, Kentucky.

After the fire had burned itself out and the smoke had dissipated, the city of Cincinnati had the remaining rubble hauled away and the lot cleared. Dirt was spread out, and trees and grass were planted along the narrow lot where the orphanage had stood only a couple months before.

It wasn't long, though, before the city began to field complaints from neighbors that the stench of the fire—its smoke and that of burning flesh—could still be smelled along the lot (now known as "the Point of Immeasurable Sorrow"). The smell was so strong that some people would choke when they walked into the lane beside the field, like their own lungs and mouths were filling up with an acrid stench, even though the new grass and budding trees had already covered up where the orphanage dormitory had once been.

But the caustic smell of the smoke was only part of the totality of the complaints. Folks were also complaining of the haunting ghostly voices: the cries of children screaming for help that never came, the voices of the sisters panicking in the confusion, the agonizing sounds of helplessness in the raging inferno.

Chapter Fifteen: St. Mary's Graveyard (Cincinnati) A Sense of Immeasurable Sorrow

The voices and the stench of burned flesh were not just limited to the grounds of the former orphanage, but they could also be experienced at the site of each of the victim's graves in both St. Mary's Cemeteries. For many who witnessed the fire, it was all very real, but to some of the neighbors, it was all in their minds. Simply grief playing jokes on the senses. They had been at the orphanage during the tragedy. They had seen and heard those terrifying events, and they thought that they just couldn't get the morose memories out of their consciousness.

Time passed and the cruel calendar turned its lonely pages. Eventually, the people who had witnessed the fire that night all died of one thing or another. Still, though, the acrid smell of burnt smoke lingers in the air, and the voices of the children can still be heard dangling in the tender ears of those not even born when the flames erupted.

If you dare to go to the site of the orphanage, you'll see that most of the area around the "Point of Immeasurable Sorrow" has long been abandoned. The place where the orphanage stood is now an empty field of overgrown weeds and untrimmed trees. In an age more superstitious than our own, no one dared to build on the site that was, if only for a few hours, someone's grave. Its natural beauty has an aura of sadness that lingers over it like a funeral shroud. History says that some of the foundation can still be found in the field, but more than charred bricks remain of the old orphanage. You will, if you have the nerve to stay a few minutes longer, start to notice that the place has a strange pungent smell and that it is still haunted by the voices of the victims.

Visit, if you can, the graves of the victims in St. Mary's Cemetery. Stand at the graves long enough and you may find yourself choking on the thick smoke of Cincinnati's tragic history. Listen long and hard, and you may hear the cries for help from beyond the grave.

CHAPTER SIXTEEN

St. Mary's Graveyard

(Cincinnati)
What's Haunting St. Mary's Graveyard?

Many visitors to St. Mary's have experienced for themselves the strange unexplained occurrences that plague this otherwise bucolic graveyard.

Saint Mary's Graveyard sits along a beautiful stretch of East Ross Avenue. Its pristine white gates and bucolic views deceive the casual visitor into thinking it's a place of rest for those departed from this earth. Those driving or walking by may see this as a tranquil place, but the story is quite different for those who live near the rather large graveyard.

My wife and I were walking one evening down East Ross Avenue when a couple working in their front yard waved at us. We waved back and stopped for a moment to chat. After exchanging pleasantries, we began a real conversation about the neighborhood. We told them that we were researching the cemeteries of Cincinnati, with an emphasis on their hauntings. Little did we know it then, but we were about to get a firsthand account of the haunting at St. Mary's Graveyard.

The older couple, the Smiths, told us that they had lived in their house for many years, but if they had known then what they know now, they would never have purchased the house. I drew my eyebrows in close as a look of bewilderment took over my face. My wife asked them what they meant. The story we got from them I am going to share with you now.

It was in early April 1986, that the Smiths started looking at the small house on East Ross Avenue. Their boys had gone off to college, and they needed a smaller place now that it was just the two of them. It was their real estate agent who first mentioned to them that some folks in the neighborhood thought that St. Mary's was haunted. At first, they just laughed it off as a bunch of crazy stories. Besides, they liked the idea that living across the street from a graveyard would be quiet and peaceful.

Without reservation they bought the house. Their first few nights in the house were filled with unpacking and a couple of long strolls through the graveyard across the street. They wanted to get to know their neighbors . . . so to speak.

But, not long after they moved in, they began to learn that the graveyard was, in fact, not as peaceful as it seemed in the daylight. Their first month in the house was quiet.

"We now call that our period of grace," the old man said.

They heard their first frightening sounds echoing throughout the house about five weeks after they occupied it. The disquiet woke them both up. They followed the oddly incessant noise all around the house, thinking it was perhaps a burglar. Soon, though, they traced the sounds out the front door and down the walkway towards the street. As they stood on the street facing the graveyard, the sound was almost deafening. They walked across the road and stood at the graveyard gates listening intensely to the indistinguishable sound emanating from the tombs beyond the gate. It was not like any other noise they had ever heard before. Were these the machinations of some nefarious spirit?

As dark storm clouds rolled in, they began to make out an odd light coming from across the graves. In time, the amorphous light began to coalesce into an eerie shaft of energy that seemed to have no source or form. The light glided across the cemetery—right towards them. As it approached, they recoiled, capitulating in fear. Then it was gone. The night was silent as well. The couple agreed they were having a mutual nightmare and decided to head back to the house. The next morning they couldn't help but feel silly at the prior night's events. They had no empirical evidence that what they had experienced was the truth. Surely they were letting a story get the best of them.

Over the next several days, they asked their neighbors if they had seen or heard anything strange at St. Mary's Graveyard. None of them had seen or heard anything that they would describe as out of the ordinary. One neighbor mentioned that they had seen a small group of kids playing there after dark, but this was nothing unusual. The neighborhood seemed quiet for the time being. The Smiths went on about their daily lives.

It was exactly one week later when the Smiths were again woken from sleep by strange sounds that seemed to be emanating from the graveyard across the street. They sat up in bed and listened as a creeping terror swelled within their hearts. What could it be? Were they just paranoid after last week's disturbing disruption?

Mr. and Mrs. Smith finally got up out of bed, got dressed, and began to look around. They first searched through the house and then on the front lawn. They were both drawn to the graveyard, pulled into it by some unseen force. Before they knew what was happening to them, they were standing inside the gates of St. Mary's Graveyard. The ominous sounds that had driven them from their bed were still swirling around them in some unintelligible audio vortex. The darkness of the night sky soon gave way to colorful lights dancing around them as if they were caught in a kaleidoscope-drenched dream. Mrs. Smith's hair flew around her head as if she were standing in a tornado that couldn't make up its mind which way to turn. The whole thing seemed surreal. The Smiths, frightened by the turn of events, didn't know whether they were in any actual danger or not. Was this just a weird experience, or were they about to pay some karmic toll for a resentment of the universe's making?

The weirdness continued for the Smiths for several more minutes before it left them lying on the grass in front of a large monument. They were exhausted and deeply frightened.

The Smiths went on to explain that similar occurrences had befallen them many more times in the years that they lived on East Ross Avenue. "The strange sightings we've had in that graveyard have, for us, never abated," Mr. Smith said. "I guess the weirdest part for me has been the fact that none of the neighbors have seen any of it; to them the neighborhood is a quiet and peaceful place to reside." Mrs. Smith just nodded her head in agreement.

"Why did you two decide to stay in the house if the graveyard across the street was haunted?" I asked the Smiths.

"It has never physically hurt us, and we love the house. So why move? I mean, anyplace one lives is going to have its pros and cons; it's just that our con is a haunted graveyard."

"Well!" I exclaimed.

"That is an amazing story, Mr. and Mrs. Smith!" Nancy said to them. "Thank you so much for sharing your experience with the haunting of St. Mary's Graveyard."

"You're welcome, and enjoy your writing" they chimed as we began to stroll off down the street.

No sooner were we out of sight of the Smith's house than Nancy turned to me and asked, "What do you make of that?"

I replied, "It was plausible, given all the strange stories I've been told over the years; but I want to see if we can get something out of one of the neighbors as it relates to their story."

A few houses down the street we stopped to ask some neighbors, a middle-aged couple sitting on their front porch, what they thought about the haunting of St. Mary's Graveyard. They looked at us as if we were crazy.

"We don't know any Smiths, and we've lived on this street a lot of years," said the gentleman. The woman chimed in that she could not recall any neighbors like the Smiths, or any house that we described to them.

"Are you sure you know everyone on this street?" I asked.

"Yeah," they replied in unison.

"Well, thank you anyway," we said before departing their company.

Nancy and I strolled back down the street to the Smith's house a few doors away. We spent over an hour looking for the house we had just visited. We evaluated each house along the street carefully, but we couldn't find it . . . or the Smiths. The Smiths, and their house, had simply vanished in the warm June air.

CHAPTER SEVENTEEN

St. Mary's Graveyard

(Ft. Mitchell, Kentucky)
A Well-Dressed Ghost

The shawl left behind by a fleeing woman is now believed to be in the possession of the well-dressed ghost.

The wandering paths and majestic beauty of St. Mary's Cemetery make it a wonderful place to take an afternoon stroll. Its bucolic setting seems more like a park than a graveyard. For as long as anyone can remember, St. Mary's has served as a resting place for the dead—and for the living.

As the maple trees began to turn a brilliant orange and the days of autumn drew shorter, William and Nellie Pierce decided to have a picnic at St. Mary's graveyard. They packed their basket, hooked the carriage to the horses, and began their short trip. Along the way they bantered back and forth about the children, the upcoming Halloween holiday, and getting the garden ready for the winter. It was a bumpy road, and the two bottles of root beer they had with them clinked together as they rode. They arrived at the graveyard just after noon.

Nellie remarked that it was a bit chilly and pulled her shawl up around her neck. William smiled lovingly at her and shook the lapel of his jacket, saying in reply, "That's why I wore my thicker jacket. I don't see how that open knit would keep anyone warm."

They spread out the red and white checkered picnic blanket and set the basket down. When they were seated on the blanket they both looked around at the lovely, peaceful setting. William and Nellie unpacked the basket and began to eat their lunch over a playful conversation on a variety of topics. They waved at other folks who were walking by where they were sitting.

Just as they were finishing up their lunch, the sun came out, and it started to get a little warmer. Nellie pulled her cloak off her shoulders and laid it down beside her. William loosened his collar and remarked that if it got any warmer he would need to take his jacket off. The couple finished their sugar pie, and Nellie curled up in William's arms as they enjoyed the rustling of the leaves and the singing of the birds. They sipped the last of their root beer and giggled softly at each other. They took out a deck of cards and had played for almost an hour when William finally stood up and said he needed to go find the privacy of the bushes at the edge of the graveyard.

Nellie replied, "I'll wait here."

William then walked off towards the heavily wooded area that ran along the wrought-iron fence. Nellie continued to look around. A few minutes later she decided that it was getting chilly again. She reached for her shawl, but it was gone. Had William taken it for some reason? she thought to herself. She could have sworn she put it right beside her, but it was gone now. Could one of the other people in the graveyard have taken it? Had it blown away in the wind? Nellie looked around, only to see an empty graveyard.

At that moment, she suddenly saw the hazy outline of a woman about her size walking away from her. The woman appeared to be wearing a shawl that was similar to the one she was missing. She shouted out to the woman, but the woman kept on moving away. Nellie got up to try and catch the woman, but by the time she got to her feet, the woman had disappeared into the mid-afternoon haze.

William returned to find Nellie in a state of confusion. "Do you remember that I took my shawl off a little while ago?" she asked William.

"Yes," he replied.

"Well, I put it beside me, and when I went to look for it again, it was gone. I thought you might have taken it, but I see you did not. I also just saw a woman wearing what looked like my shawl strolling away over that hill," Nellie said, nearly in tears. "I've lost my shawl, the one my mother made for me last Christmas."

William replied, "We'll look for it."

They both searched the picnic site as well as the carriage. The overgarment was gone.

"Well," said William, "let's pack up the basket and stroll around the graveyard here and see if we can find that woman you think might have your shawl."

A few paces down the hill they saw a woman off in the distance. "Is that her?" asked William as he lit his pipe.

"Why, yes, it is!" exclaimed Nellie.

But by the time they reached her, she had vanished into the afternoon fog. They spent another hour looking for the elusive woman, but failed to find her again.

"Tell you what," said William, "I've got to come back this way tomorrow to bring some papers to the courthouse. Why don't I stop in at the office here and see if anyone dropped it off as missing."

Nellie agreed.

Bright and early the next morning, William kissed Nellie and the children goodbye for the day. Nellie reminded him to stop off at the graveyard and ask about her shawl.

"I will," he said with a reassuring tone in his voice. William waved to his mother-in-law across the street as he got into the carriage. She waved back. His head was filled with questions as he rode along the rugged road to St. Mary's graveyard. "What could have become of that shawl?" he asked himself. "…and who was the woman that vanished into the fog?" He shook his head at the mystery of the missing shawl. He was so distracted by the shawl that he nearly forgot his business at the courthouse. When he was done at the courthouse, he immediately went to the caretaker's office at St. Mary's.

Once there, he asked the manager if anyone had turned in a missing cloak.

"It's so funny you would ask that." The manager smiled. "You're the eighth or ninth person in the last three weeks to have asked if an item of woman's clothing or an accessory has been turned in as missing here at the graveyard."

William looked puzzled. "You mean to tell me there have been other reports of women's clothes gone missing?"

"Yes," replied the manager with a chuckle.

"Do you think you have a thief strolling the grounds? My wife and I saw a woman walking around wearing a shawl that looked just like hers, but by the time we got to her she had vanished into thin air . . . like a ghost."

The manager's jovial attitude about it all of a sudden turned tepid. The smile fell off his face, and it was replaced with a sobering stare. He looked at William and asked, "So, you've seen her, too?"

"Why, yes," replied William. "My wife and I both saw her yesterday, near the crest of the hill." His thoughts were growing more bewildered as the conversation went on.

"Well," sighed the cemetery manager, "I only believed in one ghost, The Holy Ghost, that is . . . until I saw her the other day. You see, I was standing just on that ridge over there, when I saw a woman running across the cemetery not twenty feet in front of me. She appeared to drop something as she ran, and when I looked down I saw a shawl lying on the ground. Then this ghostly woman appeared . . . I tell you, I was stunned. And when I looked down again, the shawl was gone . . . and so was the ghostly figure." He shook his head in embarrassment. "I think she's been stealing all the clothes that the women have said have gone missing. I think we have a well-dressed ghost."

"A well-dressed ghost!" laughed William.

"Yes, sir, I do believe we've got a well-dressed ghost stealing the clothes of the living." Neither man could help but laugh. "I'm real sorry your wife got her cloak nicked, but it sure is funny."

William had to agree.

CHAPTER EIGHTTEEN

Vine Street Hill Cemetery

Dr. Aljuzza

Although his body is buried in the Evergreen Cemetery (formerly the Newport Cemetery) in Campbell County, Kentucky, in the shadow of Cincinnati, the ghost of Dr. Aljuzza is believed to still be wandering through Vine Street Hill Cemetery, searching for his killer.

Dr. Belam Aljuzza was a physician who practiced in Cincinnati at the end of the nineteenth century. He was known as distinctive for sporting a long moustache curled upwards at the ends and a long, pointed Van Dyke-style goatee. He was also known for the long greatcoat with cape he always wore. His medicine bag was constantly in his possession, as well as a stout black cane with a large silver pommel on top. A flashy dresser, his outfits often included brightly colored ascots and a large glittering fob dangling down from his pocket-watch chain.

Dr. Aljuzza was, in addition to being a physician and a man of high society, somewhat of a good-time aficionado. Cincinnati was a rougher city in those days. It was a working riverfront town of great geo-economic importance. Men who worked along the docks and wharfs and the nearby industries would flood the bars and whorehouses on weekends, looking for a drink and the company of loose women. There was enough money from the ramblers and the politicians, even in those days, to keep the seedy establishments and brothels open late. Bourbon flowed as freely as the Ohio River and moral malleability was easily bought and sold. Dr. Aljuzza, though married, loved every minute of it. There are those who say that the majority of his medical services were applied to treating the various social diseases that almost always came along with the city's unseemly side.

All of this came to an end for Dr. Aljuzza in 1906, though, when he walked into a bar just across the street from the Vine Street Hill Cemetery, a place called The Tavern. In a most remarkable case of ill timing, Dr. Aljuzza happened to eye a young lady who caught his fancy—a gorgeous blonde, curvy in all the right places. The sparkle in her eyes was enough to drive a man mad with avidity. He ordered a drink and slammed it in one motion before starting to make his way across the bar to where the lady sat. Just then, he noticed a man put his arm around her and make advances as she tried in vain to push him off.

Dr. Aljuzza immediately shouted out loud to the man, "Sir, I suggest you find a more willing woman to foist your affections upon!"

The man whirled around to face Dr. Aljuzza. Aljuzza pulled his cane up into a ready position as the two men stared at each other. Then, in the flash of time, the burly man lunged at Dr. Aljuzza. Several blows were exchanged before the barkeep managed to pull the large man off Dr. Aljuzza. The man, who was not known in that particular bar, rushed out the door and off into the darkness of the night. Witnesses reported seeing him flee across the street and into the Vine Street Hill Cemetery. Dr. Aljuzza lay bleeding profusely on the barroom floor. He had been stabbed in the heart by the man during the fight. He died almost instantly, right there on the cold, wooden, and beer-and-spit-soaked floor.

Dr. Aljuzza's killer was never identified or caught. His body was buried the next week in the Evergreen Cemetery (formerly the Newport Cemetery) in Campbell County, Kentucky, on the outskirts of Cincinnati.

Dr. Aljuzza's killer made his escape among the monuments and trees in Vine Street Hill Cemetery.

The Tavern was burned to the ground in a case of arson just over a year after the fatal stabbing had occurred. But, ever since that night, people have reported seeing a strange ghostly figure walking along Vine Street and through the Vine Street Hill Cemetery, near where The Tavern used to stand. He's said to be an oddly familiar figure, wearing a long greatcoat and sporting a distinguished-looking moustache and Van Dyke-style goatee. He carries an old-fashioned black physician's bag and a cane with a silver pommel on its head. The ghostly figure seems to have a purpose, a mission of some type, and carries himself that way. People for more than a hundred years have told stories of hearing the disturbing sound of the tip of a cane tapping against the pavement as the figure walks.

People who live near the Vine Street Hill Cemetery believe the shadowy figure to be that of the ghost of Dr. Aljuzza. It is always described consistently. Perhaps it is looking for the man who stabbed him that fateful night so many years ago, or perhaps it is looking for the woman who caught his eye. Some locals also say the ghost of Dr. Aljuzza's wife can sometimes be seen creeping up behind it, looking to see for herself whether its search is for the latter.

Chapter Eighteen: Vine Street Hill Cemetery Dr. Aljuzza

Vine Street Hill Cemetery, eternal home of legendary funk guitarist, Phelps "Catfish" Collins, known for his work in Parliament, Funkadelic, and Bootsy's Rubber Band.

CHAPTER NINETEEN

Walnut Hills Cemetery

Ghost in the Fireplace

The burial obelisk of Jacob Woelfle, whose strange story has become entombed in Cincinnati folklore.

It is true that many people are enchanted by the radiant glow of a fire burning in the fireplace. We are at once mesmerized by the flickering light, watching the flames dance around and casting their shadows in irregular patterns across the floor and walls. The warmth keeps us comfortable on a cold winter's night. We read books, and hold long, important conversations by its light. The fireplace, with its soft popping sound and warm feeling, has a reputation for being romantic. Many glasses of wine have been sipped by the fire's light, and many marriage proposals have been made in the fire's presence. Although our modern homes are filled with every conceivable convenience, most of us still like to have a fireplace to kindle now and again.

In the years before electricity came into our homes, the fire was the hub of the home; meals were cooked there and clothes were dried out at its margins. It was an invaluable source of heat and light, but also of danger and frightening fascination. The fire was not a toy; there was a very real potential that if one was not careful with it, the fire might set loose its wrath and engulf one's home.

While fire is widely known for both its practical and romantic uses, it also has a reputation far more nefarious. For some people, fire is a thing of evil. A place where sinister spirits dwell. A place of insanity. One can, in the otherwise dark of the night, almost feel oneself going mad staring into the endless whipping of the flames. Despite its producing light, fire has an allure that draws us to the other side. Fire is the central tenet of the occult, of dark magic and spells.

Folks along the Ohio River around Cincinnati say the fireplace is a portal, a gateway to Hell. They say that the wood you see being consumed in the flames is really but a door; that the flames are actually coming up through the earth from below. Far below. All the way from the depths of Hades, the realm of Satan.

. . . And they should know, for on a typically chilly night in April 1879, evil came to Cincinnati, came up from the vastness below; and what started as an ordinary fire in an ordinary fireplace on an ordinary night . . . soon became an inferno of terror.

It all began one evening when Jacob Woelfle went to add another log to his fire. Jacob was well known around town for being a no-nonsense businessman originally from Germany. He was what one might describe as *"Tapferer Kerl"* [stout fellow] in character, were one to be polite about it. An impolite description might run along the lines of *"Schroff"* [harsh]. He was simply just not the kind of man to make merry or go socializing much—not a bad man, just a bit coarse. His wife, Willamina, loved him dearly, and his two children admired him, even if the three of them were always a bit careful not to cross him too much. More than a few townsfolk, too, had run amok of Jacob Woelfle. He had in his day let his anger and abrupt nature upset more than one person around town. While most would acknowledge that he had done some good works, he was beginning to get a reputation as someone one might want to avoid.

According to the legend, he tossed the log onto the flames in a rather violent manner, sending sparks and embers up into the air and out across the room. Jacob was thrown back and to the floor. The fire hissed and spat for several minutes before the whole fireplace became engulfed in a thick gray smoke. Flames leapt up, and the once-bucolic fireplace had become wildly out of control. Jacob dug his fingers into the hardwood floor in fright. "What have I done?" he thought to himself as the smoke and flames raged. His head began to swirl, and he started to choke as the cloud of ashes overtook him. He saw only darkness just before he passed out.

When he came to consciousness a few minutes later, he found himself staring up at a strange ghostly figure. Not the usual diaphanous form of most ghosts, though, no, this figure seemed to be on fire. Red, orange, yellow, and blue flames crept up its figure and out its arms in slow motion, as if time had been suspended. Embers of glowing sparks emitting from its head, it wore around its shoulders a cape of dark slithering smoke. Oddly, it did not radiate heat, and only the strangest of light. It billowed and roiled like flames leaping up to catch the air. Jacob Woelfle was terrified.

He scrambled to gather his thoughts. What was this thing before him? What did it want of him? Had he provoked it, or brought it forth? His mind swirled in fear. Herr Woelfle glanced over at his wife who was sewing in the chair just across the room. She seemed at perfect peace, blissfully unaware of the occurrences rapidly unfolding before her. It was as if she saw nothing out of the ordinary in the room before her. He turned back to the fiery figure before him. The figure bent down over Jacob and extended its arms outward, stretching its fingers of fire beyond any reality that Jacob could fathom.

The ghost extended his hands out over Jacob and said, "When you violently threw that log on the fire, you smashed it against my door; you, Jacob Woelfle, aroused me . . . your anger!" The ghost glowed a frightful hue of red. "I am your anger come up from the depths of Hell! I have come to show you what anger brings, what contempt for one's fellows can bring a man. Hell and damnation is all that anger can render. There is nothing in Hell more destructive than anger! Look, I say, at your dedicated wife, Willamina . . . at how she suffers from the coarseness you often show her, and yet she loves you still. The fear you now feel at my presence is the same fear you instill in others when you show them anger. Do you understand?" cried the fiery ghost.

"Oh, great ghost of fire, spare me your wrath . . . I beg of you . . . for I had no idea what my anger was doing!" Quivering, Jacob tugged at his shirt sleeve between his teeth. The fiery ghost erupted in flares of flames, nearly engulfing the room.

The ghost replied, "I am your anger, and only you can spare yourself of your own rage. You are the only one who can control me, and I'd suggest you do before I burn your house down and take your family with me back to Hell. Now do you understand?"

Jacob replied, "Yes, I see now!" The flames emanating from the inferno at last began to die down.

"Never forget, Jacob Woelfle, when destruction subsides, when anger calms, a chance for something new appears." The specter slowly receded back into the fireplace, and disappeared into the glowing embers of a dying fire. Jacob again passed out, falling back onto the floor in front of the fireplace.

When he at last awoke he found himself lying in his own bed. The sheets were pulled up around him, and his wife was sitting on the end of the bed. Their two children, Abigail and Charlie, were standing by with smiles on their faces. The morning sun was beginning to peek through the window, the cock was crowing, and the calendar had turned a page.

Jacob sat up in bed, and as he opened his eyes to the wonderful sight before him, Jacob Woelfle reached out and hugged his wife and children. He hugged them tight, and with all the love a husband and father could muster. Tears of gratitude poured down his face. The four of them just sat holding each other as if they were all they each had.

Willamina finally said, "You gave us quite a fright last night. I looked up from my sewing and saw you passed out on the hardwood floor in front of the fireplace. I thought you might have hurt yourself, and I'm overjoyed to see you alive and well this morning."

Jacob replied, "I suppose I was hurting myself in a way, but I'm afraid what I was really doing was hurting you three. I never want to hurt you again. Please find it in your hearts to forgive me of my anger."

Willamina replied, "Of course."

"I have sent my discontent back to Hell where it belongs . . . and I feel like a new man, free of his greatest burden. C'mon everyone, let's pack a picnic and go explore Cincinnati as a family."

Jacob Woelfle and Willamina lived a long happy life along with their two children. Jacob continued to be a successful businessman and a respected and revered member of his community. The fiery ghost never appeared to Jacob, or anyone else, ever again.

Jacob and Willamina are resting peacefully together in Walnut Hills Cemetery in Cincinnati, Ohio.

CHAPTER TWENTY

Walnut Hills Cemetery

Till Death Do Us Rest

These two headstones in Walnut Hills Cemetery
tell of a love story from beyond the grave.

Friederich Würth Sr. ran a construction company in Wiesbaden, Hesse, Germany, and it enjoyed tremendous growth in the years after the consolidation of the German Confederation in 1815. For several years the family made money and achieved a comfortable status in the area. Friederich Würth Sr. was an adroit businessman but also a family man. In 1821, he and his wife welcomed their first baby boy. They named him Friederich Würth Jr. after his father. Two years later, they had a little girl and named her Anna.

By 1828, though, the political climate in Hesse, Germany was changing. The first signs of a political reassignment were starting to appear, and Friederich Würth Sr. wanted to get out before his company was upended. In 1829, he and his family emigrated to a burgeoning German community in Cincinnati, Ohio, known as "Over the Rhine."

Not long after the Würth family settled in Cincinnati, Mrs. Würth had another son. Friedrich was proud of his growing family and they were as close-knit as a family could be. He continued to work in the construction industry, taking on his eldest son as an apprentice. Friedrich Würth learned quickly and grew strong. At the age of twenty-three, he met a young lady from the neighborhood who had the feminine version of his own name, Friedericka. On the day they met, they could not stop laughing at their names—Friederich and Friedericka—it was quite amusing to all. They soon went a courting.

Friederich and Friedericka were married in the Lutheran Church of Cincinnati in the spring of 1845. He was, by that time, a skilled carpenter in his own right, and Friedericka was ready to begin raising a family of her own. The two were inseparable. Theirs was a marriage straight out of a romance novel. The two of them were madly in love. The long days of summer were spent sitting on the hills looking out over the Ohio River, while the cold nights of winter were spent by the fireplace. They were not, though, without their trials, for in late 1846, they lost an infant son due to an uncontrollable fever. The next year, Friederich lost both his mother and his father within a few months. Whatever the tragedy, they always seemed to triumph. Together, they eventually raised two boys, John and Lucien, as well as three girls, Maude, Claire, and Sarah. As the years passed, they saw their children and their love grew even stronger. A bit later, Friederich and Friedericka saw both their boys go off to fight for the Union Army with the 1st Ohio Infantry. The years of the Civil War were hard on them, but, as always, they persevered. Friedericka looked forward to receiving letters from her two boys, letters that were too few and far apart. Both boys made it back alive and followed in their father's footsteps, apprenticing with their father from the late 1860s onward. Two of the three girls married after the war and raised families of their own.

In late March of 1877, the Würths celebrated their thirty-second wedding anniversary. A few days later, Friederich fell very ill. He was bed ridden by the first of April and unable to work. Friedericka would spend hours wiping his brow and cleaning him up. She fed him in bed and sat up with him all night if need be. There were moments when he appeared to be getting better, but mostly he was declining. He was diagnosed with pneumonia accompanied by a high fever. Despite the best efforts of both Friedericka and the doctors, he died from his illness on April 28, 1877.

He was laid to rest in the Walnut Hills Cemetery, and a marker was erected to him by his widow. Immediately after the burial, Friedericka began to visit the grave regularly. She would tell friends of how she and Friederich used to stroll the graveyard on Sunday afternoons, a Victorian-era tradition they favored. Her friends and family noticed that she was in a deep state of mourning. She sewed herself a simple black dress to wear to the cemetery.

It wasn't long, though, before she began to speak to her friends of her husband's ghost. She would describe the ghost of Friederich as sitting with her at the grave while they spoke of the children and their love. Her friends were bemused when she began to talk of their Sunday strolls in the present tense, as if she and Friederich were still enjoying them together. Most of those around her simply thought that this was a phase, that she was mourning and that it would soon pass. It didn't.

Week after week went by and all Friedericka would do was sit at Friederich's grave and talk with his ghost. She claimed that he spoke with her, too. "Das klingt geheimnisvoll," [that sounds mysterious] her friends would reply to her. In Victorian times, it was normal and accepted for a widow to spend exactly one year mourning the loss of a husband. Any mourning beyond that was not displayed in public. But, for Friedericka, more than a year went by, and still she sat at the grave day after day talking with a ghost only she could see. All anyone else saw was Friedericka sitting or strolling alone talking to herself. Her children, although they had sympathy for her loss, began to discuss putting her into an asylum. Her two sons were ready to commit her, but the girls were reluctant; they thought maybe she would come out of it. None of the children believed in ghosts, much less their father's ghost. They all claimed that their mother was either in a deep state of mourning, or that she was going insane. Eventually, though, as her odd behavior continued, all her children faced the fact that Friedericka was descending into madness. She was simply not getting back to normal. All she spoke of was the ghost of Friederich by her side. It was as if she had died as well. The children missed their father, but did not believe that his ghost was haunting Walnut Hills Cemetery.

In 1881, the decision was made to commit her to the local asylum. She was given a private room and a nurse. At first the doctors at the asylum felt that she just needed a long rest, a chance to think about and do something else. She was invited to join a sewing circle and a gardening club. The doctors thought that these activities would be good for her. At first she seemed to relax, but soon she took a turn for the worse. Late one night, she was heard screaming hysterically through her window. When the nurses arrived they found her clinging to the bars on her window shouting about her husband, who was walking around outside in the moonlight. The staff searched the grounds to assuage her, but, of course, Friederich was not found. After that she continued to spiral downward into all sorts of supernatural obsessions. She would hold séances in her room and spend hours reading about necromancy and divination. She continued to claim that the ghost of Friederich was with her. The doctors tried to get through to her but to no avail. Soon, she began to talk as if she too were a ghost. Friedericka Würth had lost all contact with the living, with reality. Even when her children visited, all she could ask them was, "Have you brought your father with you today?" Slowly, little by little, the children quit visiting their mother. It was just too painful for them.

The next two years passed without any improvement. By the time 1884 rolled around, Friedericka was a shadow of her former self. She was a wraith of a woman.

The summer of 1884 was an especially hot and humid one in Cincinnati. The heat claimed several victims across the city, including a weakened Friedericka. She died of heat exhaustion in July of that year. Although her children were sad, they were also somewhat relieved for her. They buried her right next to their father Friederich, holding her funeral at the graveside. As her children and extended family looked on, Friedericka was lowered into the warm summer soil. The children all agreed to get together one year from that date at the graveyard. They wanted to make an annual family visit to their parents' grave.

One year to the day, in July 1885, the children of Friederich and Friedericka Würth got together again. As they stood by the dual graves, all of a sudden, the ghosts of their parents appeared. They all stared in amazement at the sight before them. Despite its impossibility, there they were, the ghostly figures of Friederich and Friedericka Würth looking lovingly at their children. Both of them appeared robust and healthy, strong and full of life. As the children watched, Friederich and Friedericka Würth locked arms and slowly began to stroll off together on a meandering walk around the graveyard grounds.

John asked, "Could we have been wrong? Could Mama have really been seeing Pa all along?"

"I don't know John; I am not mad, and yet I see them strolling now as plainly as the moonlight," replied Claire.

Whatever they had believed before, all the children could do now was agree that their parents were indeed haunting the Walnut Hills Cemetery.

This house, near the Avondale neighborhood, was once a boarding house and the scene of a grisly murder. Remnants of the victim still haunt this house even though the body was interred in Mount Moriah Cemetery. The other part of its ghostly remains roam the grounds of Mount Moriah Cemetery.

CHAPTER TWENTY-ONE

Walnut Hills Cemetery

Haunted History

The gravestone pictured here is among the most famous in Walnut Hills Cemetery. It depicts a mother mourning the loss of her two children, who are laid to rest beneath it.

Formed in February 1843, Walnut Hills Cemetery is one of the oldest burial grounds in Cincinnati. It was originally named "the Second German Protestant Cemetery," and was laid out on just over five acres of land not far from central Cincinnati. The board of director members are listed as: C. F. Bultmann, Hermann Ficke, A. Frieman, Louis Wehmer, and Charles Wolf. The first interment dates to June 30, 1843. The cemetery has accepted burials ever since. Walnut Hills Cemetery now covers over seventy acres of land, and currently has over 50,000 registered burials. Dating to the pre-Civil War era, the Second German Protestant Cemetery was originally segregated, as were most cemeteries at that time. It is now a fully integrated burial ground.

To avoid confusion with "the First German Protestant Cemetery," the name was changed to Walnut Hills Cemetery in September of 1941. Originally opened in 1802, "the First German Protestant Cemetery" (located in the 3600 block of Reading Road) was closed to interments in 1864 after many victims of the cholera outbreaks of 1849 and 1864 had been buried there. The First German Protestant Cemetery is known to be haunted of the ghosts of the two outbreaks. There have been several reports over the years of people encountering ghostly figures that displayed the evidence of cholera: sunken eyes, drawn bluish skin, wrinkles on the hands, and the stench of diarrhea. These ghostly victims are said to wander around like see-through zombies. In the years before modern medical advances had been made, many believed that handling the graves, bodies, or bones of victims would re-spread cholera.

While no cholera victims are known to have been buried in Walnut Hills Cemetery, it is no less a place of odd occurrences. The chapel is said to still contain what remains of the spirit of a young boy who died during the influenza outbreak of 1919. According to local legend, his funeral was held at the chapel. Four men, including his father, were the pallbearers. They each stated later that when they lifted the coffin at the conclusion of the funeral, that it was considerably lighter than the one they had brought in earlier that day. When they opened the coffin to see what the issue was, all they saw was the shriveled corpse of a sickly looking boy. It had, according to a diary entry from the boy's mother "lost its spirit, and what remained was only rotting flesh." The boy's body (who shall remain anonymous here) was buried in Walnut Hills that day, but his ghost remains in the chapel.

In the original African-American section of the cemetery that dates to the pre-Civil War era, there is a strange tale of supernatural proportions. In 1855, an African-American slave by the name of Josiah was buried in the Second German Protestant Cemetery by his master. He was a young man of about twenty-four years. He had most likely been a house slave, cleaning and serving meals for the family since he was a wee tot. Most slaves were buried in graves that had wooden markers that have long been lost to time. So all that is known about Josiah is a footnote in his master's journals denoting his name, death date, approximate age, and general place of burial. Over the years, though, Josiah has been seen walking around the African-American section bathed in a bright glowing light, as if he were being highlighted from the world beyond.

CHAPTER TWENTY-TWO

Cincinnati Cemeteries

Weeping Willows and Other Graveyard Symbology

A common motif in graveyards across Cincinnati and the world is the weeping willow. This gracefully pendulant tree is symbolic of weeping or mourning in the funerary tradition.

A common motif in graveyards throughout the world, weeping willows have adorned burial grounds for centuries. They are planted in the ground—themselves buried . . . so to speak—and their images carved upon headstones. Weeping willows are seen as both grandly majestic and symbolic in a cemetery setting.

The weeping willow (*Salix babylonica pendula*) is an ancient tree native to northern China, but cultivated all over Asia and Europe for millennia. The weeping willow gets its common name from the long slender flowing branches that arch upward before swooping downward to the ground. The leaves themselves are in the shape of elongated teardrops. The branches and leaves flow and sway in the slightest breeze, giving the appearance of shaking, as if sobbing lugubriously. They are said to be "weeping" in their form.

In both recent and ancient times, weeping willows were easy to find, cut, and carve. For this reason, they became the wood of choice for grave markers in rural areas, as well as along the Silk Road that stretched from Asia into Europe.

One old legend from Germany says that if you plant a weeping willow tree at a gravesite, it will spread its "mourning veil," or "*Trauer Schleier*," down over the loved one. The veil, or branches, were thought to protect the soul of the deceased from any ghosts or demons that may wish it harm in the next life. This legend came about due to the weeping willow tree forming an umbrella of branches that are easy to hide within. Cincinnati is a heavily German city, and the fact that so many weeping willows are planted in its cemeteries should surprise no one familiar with this legend.

Another legend says that if you want to see a ghost, all you need do is look under a weeping willow by the light of the full moon. There you will see the ghosts of the night trying to hide from view.

The trees' association with crying is the reason that they are commonly used in graveyards, as a symbol for mourning those who have died and been buried. Although flowers are a traditional offering to those in mourning, a weeping willow tree for planting also makes a historically traditional offering.

Other symbols commonly seen on tombstones include: winged skulls, winged hourglasses, hands shaking, upside down torches, lambs, bundles of wheat, limbless tree trunks, and broken roses. Tombstones presented as benches allow loved ones to sit at the grave and visit with those who have gone before.

Skulls have always been a symbol of death, and winged skulls are believed to be a representation of the soul being carried off to the afterlife. This particular motif embodies, or disembodies if you like, the very definition of "Gothic" as an architectural style and was popular during the pre-Victorian era (approximately 1700 to 1837). The motif can be seen on many tombstones from that time.

The winged hourglass is simply a representation of the swift and fleeting time one has in this mortal life. The wings represent the fleeting nature, while the hourglass represents time itself.

A common symbol in both Catholic and non-Catholic cemeteries, two hands shaking, has for hundreds of years been seen as a symbol of those departing this life—and those left behind. A goodbye gesture at parting, as it might be.

Inverted torches carry a much more sinister message to those above the ground. They are thought to be lighting the way to the underworld. Upside down torches are regarded by symbologists as a sign that the person is most likely in Hell. Some historians point out that anything inverted is meant to be, by its inversion, a representation of evil. These symbols were most often reserved for those who died without making a final confession, or for those who had been executed for unforgivable sins. Modern thinkers tend to regard them as a historical teaching tool to frighten churchgoers into a uniform code of behavior. A kind of "Do as we say, or you'll end up like this poor sinner"—burning in the flames of Hell for all eternity—symbol.

Lambs, most often seen on the graves of young children who have passed, symbolize innocence and purity. In some faith traditions they also represent Jesus, the Lamb of God.

A very common motif, bundles of wheat represent those taken from us in the normal course of life, a harvest reaped at maturity—the fulfillment of life and a preparation for the next phase of existence. Widely regarded as the most peaceful and loving of the graveyard symbols, bundles of wheat are the representation of a happy recognition of a life whose potential has been fulfilled.

Limbless tree trunks are a rare, but not unheard-of, motif. They simply represent a life cut short, or cut down in its prime (but usually after infancy). This symbol might appear as the gravestone of a young boy killed in a teenage accident or a woman who died in childbirth. My aunt's tombstone in Highland Cemetery is a cut-down tree branch, indicating she died before her elder years set in. Graves with limbless tree trunks are more likely, because of what they symbolize, to be haunted than other graves. Ghost seekers note that someone whose life was cut short is more likely to become a ghost than someone who dies of old age. Ghosts are often noted for being "restless." It is as if they have unfinished business in this life. Most cemetery historians and ghost seekers agree that when a life is cut short it leaves behind a restless ghost that wants to somehow finish its life, but can't.

Perhaps the rarest of the gravestone symbols covered here, a broken rose is similar to the limbless tree symbol. It indicates that death came after the person reached some stage of maturity, but died younger than might be reasonably expected. It is as if they lived long enough into the summer of their lives for the rose to blossom, but were broken off from this life before the autumn could work its seasonal changes upon the person.

There are, of course, many other symbols used to adorn or decorate gravestones. Rubbing, to attain a picture of the symbol, has long been a graveyard

A bench-style gravestone invites family and friends to visit the departed, as was much more common in days gone by. This particular gravestone is in Oak Hill Cemetery.

tradition, although one needs to get permission from the family and the graveyard before attempting to do a rubbing. Many religions have symbols that are unique to their traditions, and many people choose a personal symbol that may or may not be distinguishable to the general public. In the modern era, getting a custom symbol is a simple matter, with the possibilities nearly endless.

Conclusion

. . . And as you bury this collection of ghost stories in your memory, be sure to look over your shoulder as you whistle past the graveyard, for one never knows what may rise from the tombs among Cincinnati's haunted burial grounds. Cincinnati cemeteries are sprawling, breathtaking, and many in number. Some of their haunted history has been revealed, but many more supernatural mysteries await . . .

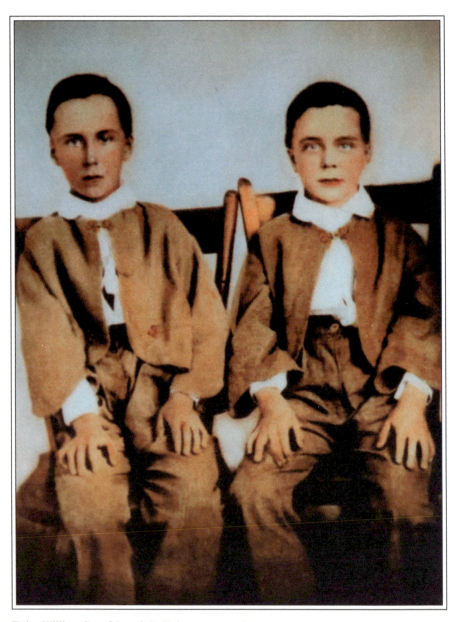

Twins William C. and Joseph B. Heizer, great uncle and grandfather of author Roy Heizer. Joseph B. Heizer is mentioned in the first story.